BEFORE YOU BEGIN…

You're about to embark on a powerful journey—a story of resilience, growth, and transformation. But this isn't just a tale. It's a roadmap for your own mastery.

Here's what others have experienced through the KT3 System:

"KT3 armed me with a tactical edge and unshakable resilience, transforming ambition into mastery and enabling me to lead with purpose and precision in every arena."
— *Raad Ajlouni, Entrepreneur*

"KT3 gave me the discipline and mindset to overcome challenges I never thought possible. It's more than training—it's transformation." — Nas Dimitroy, Holistic Healer

"Through the KT3 mentorship, I learned how to apply ancient wisdom to modern challenges. I'm now more focused and confident than ever." — Rose Nguyen, Executive

"KT3 taught me how to grow continuously and overcome obstacles I never thought I could." — Annie Newman. Holistic Healer

If you've ever felt stuck, unsure of your path, or weighed down by obstacles that seem impossible to overcome, you're not alone. But with KT3, you'll find clarity, strength, and a roadmap to your personal mastery.

As you read, **imagine yourself** applying these lessons:
Absorb wisdom.
Train with discipline.
Grow into your strongest, most focused self.

A MESSAGE FROM MASTER WONG

I didn't come from privilege or education. I came from the streets—"Bụi Đời"—where survival was my only focus. But through belief in myself and the wisdom of three great mentors—Master Chien, Master Linh, and Master Lee—I transformed my life. They taught me that hardship can either break you or build you, depending on how you face it.

As Master Chien would often say: "Kiếp Nghèo Ôm Hận"—poor fortune breeds hatred. But I realized that we don't have to let hardship make us bitter. Instead, we can use it to become stronger. Master Chien showed me how to master my mind and conquer fear. Master Lee taught me the importance of tactical training in life, and Master Linh guided me to understand that real transformation comes from within.

These lessons became the foundation of the KT3 System—Knowledge Transfer (KT), Tactical Training (TT), and Transformational Growth (TG). This system helped me rise from nothing to become Master Wong, now sharing my journey with over 5 millions of followers across the world.

If I can do this—with no formal education, starting from nothing—so can you. Your struggles don't define you, but how you rise above them does. This book is not just a story; it's an invitation to believe in yourself and your own potential. Your journey, like mine, begins with belief. If you believe in yourself, there's nothing you can't overcome.

"Before we master the world, we must first master ourselves. The greatest battles are not fought with fists, but with the mind, the spirit, and the heart." — Master Wong

As You Enter the Journey,

Believe in your power to transform. Mastery starts with…

The purity of your intent.

The focus of your will.

The level of your awareness.

The quality of your character.

With belief as your foundation, your journey begins.

—Master Wong

By the time you finish this book, you'll be ready to begin your own KT3 transformation. The next step is already within your reach, and **your journey can start today**.

www.kt3system.com

The way you do anything is the way you do everything.

Start now—begin mastering your life with KT3.

WHAT READERS SAY

"This book is a combination of the Karate Kid and Rocky. Master Wong is a combination of Daniel Son and Rocky Balboa. This is the ultimate in what martial arts is all about."
GRANDMASTER - John Hackleman (Pit Master)
Founder of The Pit Hawaiian Kempo

"A very good story, well written and interesting. It's easy to get absorbed in the story and forget it is about Master Wong's early life. I'm looking forward to more in the future"
GRANDMASTER - Samuel Kwok
Traditional Ip Man Wing Chun

"Good book, great story, a tough life journey."
Will Henshaw
World of Martial Arts Television

"An inspirational story of self-discipline and self-motivation. Master Wong goes from 'Coming from NOTHING' to 'Becoming SOMETHING'!"
Sal Mascoli
IDO Consulting

"It's powerful yet liberating, leaving you Tormented yet cleansed - wanting to read more."
Jazz Gill
Founder / CEO - SPARBAR®

"Awesome page-turning narrative. Raw, open and gripping."
Paul "Chuck" Norris
Bush Adventures UK C.I.C

THE RECKONING
Little Dragon

By Master Wong

Copyright © 2019 All rights reserved.

THE RECKONING
Little Dragon
Table of Contents

FOREWORD

It has been my privilege to know Master Wong for many years, initially as my teacher and later as a close family friend. I regard his family as my own, and I am honored to contribute this foreword to his remarkable book.

Before delving into the story of young Hung and the central theme of bullying, I must first speak of the man, Master Wong. In my 40 years of involvement in martial arts, I have encountered many senior, world-class practitioners across various disciplines. Among them, Master Wong stands out as the real deal. He possesses deep knowledge and the ability to put that knowledge into practice. He has lived through the challenges he teaches about.

This book vividly recounts the trials and tribulations of young Hung, who, from the tender age of six, endured unimaginable beatings from local gangs and, at times, from his own mother. While some of the punishment from his mother might have been deserved—though perhaps not to the extent it was delivered—the brutality of his early life is heart-wrenching.

Reflecting on my own childhood at ages six and seven, I recall the worst offense I committed was a loud fart in class, for which I failed to take responsibility, resulting in the entire class being kept in detention. Even then, my classmates did not hold it against me. It wasn't until I was around eleven years old that I experienced any form of bullying—when I was subjected to a judo stomach throw by the school bully.

The reasons behind Hung's suffering are clear: the pervasive fear in his community, the power dynamics exploited by the bullies, and his ethnicity. These factors, both in the past and in different forms today, continue to affect many in our society. Bullying manifests in various forms—physical and mental—and can occur anywhere: at home, on the streets, in school, at play, and at work. While being prepared to defend oneself is crucial, there is also wisdom in avoiding trouble when possible.

This is a lesson I learned early on, and it has served me well, leading to only one real fight in my life. However, when your back is against the wall, or your loved ones are in danger, sometimes you must fight.

Like Master Wong, I have no tolerance for bullies. If this book helps even one young person to recognize and navigate the dangers around them, then Master Wong will have achieved his goal by writing this powerful and gripping narrative.

TREVOR GILBERT OBE
6TH DAN KARATE - SHIHAN

DEDICATION

To my father, who gave me the strength to survive, and to Master Chien, who became a second father and guided me through the darkest times,

This book, Little Dragon: The Reckoning, is dedicated with profound love and gratitude to the two men who have shaped my life in ways words cannot fully express.

To my father,
Though our time together was brief, the lessons you imparted have lasted a lifetime. I still vividly recall the day you placed that knife in my hand—a small, worn blade that carried more weight than its size suggested. It wasn't just a tool; it was a symbol of your love, your protection, and the survival instincts you instilled in me. That knife saved my life on countless occasions, but more importantly, it was the mindset you gave me—rooted in **Knowledge Transfer (KT)** and **Tactical Training (TT)**—that kept me truly safe. You taught me that true strength comes not from the blade itself but from the mind that wields it.

Even though you weren't always physically by my side, your spirit and wisdom were ever-present. The values you instilled—courage, resilience, and the importance of strategic thinking—have guided me through every challenge life has thrown my way. I carry your lessons in my heart, and they continue to shape the man I am today.

To Master Chien,
You became the second father I needed when life was at its most difficult. In the chaos of a war-torn childhood, you welcomed me into your life and transformed my despair into hope. Your home was my sanctuary, and your teachings the

foundation upon which I built my life. I remember the long nights of training under the stars, where you taught me not just the physical art of Wing Chun and the principles of **KT3** but also the deep philosophies of **Transformational Growth (TG)**. You showed me how to turn every challenge into an opportunity for growth, how to harness the power of resilience, and how to balance life's complexities like Yin and Yang.

Your wisdom has been a guiding light, helping me navigate the treacherous paths of both the battlefield and life itself. Whether we were moving through the dense jungles of Vietnam or the urban streets, you taught me that survival goes beyond physical strength—it's about mastering the mind and spirit. Through **TG,** you taught me to grow stronger with each adversity, turning setbacks into stepping stones toward greater heights.

Your dedication to your craft and your students is a testament to your greatness, and I am forever grateful to have been under your tutelage.

To both of you, my fathers,
This book is a testament to the legacies you have left with me. It is with great honor that I dedicate Little Dragon: The Reckoning to you both. May your teachings continue to inspire and empower those who read these pages. Your commitment to excellence, resilience, and self-improvement will forever guide me and those who follow in our footsteps.

Thank you, Father, for your love and the survival instincts you gave me. Thank you, Master Chien, for being the father I needed when my own was no longer there. Your influences have made me who I am, and I hope to pass on your wisdom to the next generation.

Master Wong

ACKNOWLEDGMENT

The journey of writing this book has been deeply transformative, marked by moments of profound reflection and growth. This work would not have been possible without the unwavering support, guidance, and inspiration of many remarkable individuals who have profoundly shaped my path.

First and foremost, my deepest gratitude goes to my parents, whose values and love have always been my guiding light. To my partner, Mai, my daughter, Nikita, and my son, Vin—your unshakeable belief in me provided the bedrock upon which this book was built. Your love, wisdom, and enduring encouragement have been my greatest sources of strength and inspiration. Every word in these pages is a testament to the values you've instilled in me.

To my mentors and teachers, especially Master Chien and Master Linh, words cannot fully express my gratitude. The lessons I've learned from you extend far beyond martial arts; they have been lessons about life, resilience, and the strength of the human spirit. I still remember the day Master Chien told me, "The greatest fight is the one within." That single sentence has shaped my entire approach to both martial arts and life.

A special thank you to my KT3 co-writers, Philip and Douglas—your dedication, insight, and hard work brought this story to life. Our collaboration was not just a creative process, but a shared journey. Your contributions were invaluable, and I am deeply grateful for your partnership.

To my dear friends and colleagues at the KT3 Team—James and the rest of the team—your tireless efforts, shared passion, and commitment to this project have made this book possible.

Thank you for believing in this vision and for helping me see it through.

To the global martial arts community, whose spirit of perseverance and respect for the art form inspired much of what is contained in these pages, this book is for you. Your discipline, determination, and passion continue to inspire me daily.

Finally, to the readers—thank you. Your interest in this story and your desire to explore the worlds of martial arts and resilience have been the driving force behind my decision to share these experiences. I hope this book serves as a reminder that within every challenge lies the seed of resilience and growth—**may you discover that strength within yourself.**

Thank you all for being part of this journey.

DISCLAIMER

This book is set in the 1970s and early 1980s, depicting frequent violence and physical injury. Reader discretion is advised, and parents should consider its suitability for younger readers.

Though based on true events, some names and details have been changed for narrative flow. The story reflects the experiences of Hung, now known as Master Wong, during his difficult childhood in northern Vietnam, including repeated beatings as part of his upbringing.

Master Wong wishes to clarify that he holds no resentment toward his mother. In 1970s Vietnam, physical discipline was common, and this story portrays the reality of that time.

This book is written for a global audience. You may encounter unfamiliar words or expressions—Master Wong encourages resourcefulness in looking them up!

WARNING: The martial arts techniques in this book are dangerous and should not be attempted without proper training.

Explanation of Names: Master Wong, known as Hung during his early life in Vietnam, adopted the name "Michael" after moving to England. Vietnamese names are used in the narrative, with some Westernized nicknames where appropriate.

PROLOGUE

TIDES OF DESPERATION
The Exodus Begins Vietnam/China Border

The end of the Vietnam War in 1975 should have brought peace to a war-weary nation, but instead, it unleashed a new wave of terror across the land. The communist regime from the north took control of southern Vietnam, and what followed was chaos. Businesses were confiscated, families torn apart, and millions lived in fear of the brutal "re-education" camps. Starvation, unemployment, and violence spread like wildfire. Many saw no choice but to flee—leaving behind the only home they had ever known.

Among those affected were countless families from both the north and the south, forced to make the most difficult decision of their lives: **stay and suffer or risk everything to escape**. It was in these desperate times that the world witnessed the rise of the **Vietnamese Boat People**, a mass exodus of people who took to the seas in overcrowded boats, hoping to find safety on distant shores.

The War's Shadow

While the Vietnam War raged on for two decades, tensions with neighboring China grew. In 1979, China launched an invasion into northern Vietnam, wreaking havoc along the border. The people in these regions faced unspeakable horrors—villages were destroyed, and countless men, women, and children were killed or displaced. Amid the chaos, the fragile boats heading out to sea were not only symbols of escape but also of **desperation**.

Hung's Story

It is against this backdrop that our story begins. The exodus, the fear, the constant threat of violence—these were not just news headlines; they were the realities Hung faced as a child in northern Vietnam. The war shaped his world, and the scars of those times lingered long after the battles ended.

For Hung, the journey was more than survival. It was a fight to reclaim his identity, to navigate a life torn apart by forces beyond his control. As he watched people risk everything to flee their homeland, he too would face impossible choices, endure pain, and begin a path that would forge him into the man known today as **Master Wong**.

Setting the Stage for *Little Dragon: The Reckoning*
This book takes place in the late 1970s and early 1980s, a time of chaos and upheaval. It is the story of a boy caught in the tide of history, determined to rise above it. As Hung fights for his future, the lessons he learns through suffering, resilience, and survival will transform him into something more—a master of not only martial arts but of life itself.

*"When the waves of life crash upon us, we must
be strong enough to rise above the tide."*

INTRODUCTION

In the aftermath of the Vietnam War, a nation ravaged by decades of conflict found itself plunged into a new era of fear and uncertainty. The war may have ended, but its scars remained deeply etched into the lives of those who survived.

The struggles were no longer fought on battlefields but in the shadowy alleys and hostile villages, where survival became a daily battle against poverty, oppression, and the brutal forces of nature and humanity.

Among the many lives caught in this turmoil was a young boy named Hung. Born into a world where hope was a dangerous dream, Hung's journey would test the very limits of his endurance, courage, and spirit. His story is not just one of survival, but of transformation—a transformation driven by the relentless hardships he would face and the wisdom he would gain along the way.

From an early age, Hung's mixed heritage set him apart.

The blood of both Vietnamese and Chinese ancestors flowed through his veins, marking him as an outsider in a land torn by cultural and political strife. The taunts hurled at him—"half-breed," "outsider"—were more than just words; they were weapons, each one carving deep wounds into his psyche.

But the hatred from others was not his only enemy. Inside him, a greater battle raged: the war against fear. It threatened to consume him, to shape his every decision, his every step.

Yet, fear could be both tormentor and teacher, as Hung would learn. It could paralyze, yes, but it could also sharpen the senses, heighten awareness, and fuel survival when survival seemed impossible. In the dark alleys of his village, where danger was as constant as the air he breathed, Hung learned to anticipate threats, to understand the nuances of fear. This was not a passive education. His body bore the bruises and scars of his harsh lessons, but something stronger was forming within him—an understanding that fear, when controlled, could be a powerful weapon.

Still, Hung's knowledge did not come solely from the streets. In his early years, it was his father's quiet strength that grounded him. His father, a man hardened by the weight of a family barely surviving, imparted lessons of kindness, responsibility, and resilience. These lessons, while simple, would serve as Hung's emotional compass throughout his journey. His father's words echoed in moments of darkness, reminding him that strength wasn't just about physical survival—it was about maintaining one's humanity, even in a world that sought to strip it away.

But life was unrelenting, and as Hung's journey continued, he would encounter a different kind of mentor—a man who had faced the horrors of war firsthand. This mentor, a former resistance fighter named Master Chien, had survived the brutal realities of guerrilla warfare, where survival required more than just brute strength—it demanded strategy, patience, and the ability to see ten steps ahead of any enemy. Through flashbacks and stories, Chien would share his war-torn experiences with Hung, offering tactical wisdom forged in the crucible of conflict. Chien's lessons were not just about fighting; they were about understanding the psychological battleground of survival, a mindset that would challenge and shape Hung in ways he could never have imagined.

It was within this crucible of suffering, guided by both his father's emotional wisdom and Chien's tactical brilliance, that Hung began to transform. The beatings, the bullying, the constant threat of violence—these weren't just obstacles to overcome. They were pieces of a brutal education, teaching him to anticipate, to adapt, and to grow stronger with each challenge. Fear, once his greatest enemy, became the very thing that fueled his evolution.

And so, Hung's story is not merely one of learning to fight back. It is about learning to rise above. It is about finding the strength within to face the demons, both external and internal, that sought to destroy him. It is about transforming pain into power, fear into focus. Through the contrasting lessons of his father's moral guidance and Chien's survival tactics, Hung would come to understand that true strength was not just in the body, but in the mind and spirit. The hardships he endured would become the foundation of what he would later call the KT3 System: Knowledge Transfer (KT), Tactical Training (TT), and Transformational Growth (TG).

Set against the backdrop of a war-torn country and a society fractured by cultural and political divisions, *Little Dragon: The Reckoning* delves deep into the psyche of a young boy forced to mature far beyond his years. Through Hung's eyes, we witness a world where survival is a daily struggle, but where hope, no matter how fragile, remains a weapon more powerful than any sword or fist.

As you turn the pages of this story, prepare to be transported into the heart of a world where every day is a fight for survival. But more than that, prepare to see how the human spirit, no matter how battered, can emerge transformed on the other side. This is not just a tale of resilience; it is a roadmap for those who seek to understand how to navigate the darkest times and come out stronger, wiser, and more determined than ever before.

CHAPTER 1

DEMONS AT DAWN

"The only thing we have to fear is fear itself." — Franklin D. Roosevelt

By the time Hung reached six years old, life had already become a slow, grinding descent into personal hell. His hair, once a wild, tangled mess, had stopped growing altogether—so matted and knotted from frequent scuffles that cutting it was the only way to control it. Eventually, his head was shaved in a desperate attempt to control something in a world where everything else seemed beyond his grasp. The shaved scalp became his armor—thin, yet somehow significant in a world where everything seemed out of control.

On the morning of Hung's sixth birthday, the war between Vietnam and China raged on, tearing through villages and lives with ruthless precision. But for Hung, it was the personal war within his family that tore at him the most. His mother, a proud Vietnamese woman, and his father, a Chinese immigrant, were trapped in a silent, cultural battle—one that marked their family as outcasts in the slums of northern Vietnam. The insults hurled at Hung by the neighborhood children—taunts of "Chink-eyed" and "Half-breed"—cut deeper than any blow could. Each word left scars more lasting than physical ones, burrowing into his soul and feeding the fear that churned constantly within him.

That morning, the familiar sound of shattering glass jolted Hung awake. His body stiffened, heart pounding in his chest as his senses came alive. The crash had become so routine in the Wong household that it no longer startled him. But the knot in his stomach, that ever-tightening ball of dread, was impossible to ignore. Fear had woven itself into the fabric of his life, ever-present and suffocating. Even in sleep, it lingered, a shadow that clung to him.

Hung lay still, listening. His parents were arguing again, their voices sharp and muffled through the thin walls of the shack. His mother, resolute as always, was picking up shards of glass from the floor, while his father's curses drifted into the wind outside. Hung didn't need to fully understand their argument to know what it was about. His father had mentioned the boat again—escape.

The thought made Hung's stomach twist even tighter. He wanted to run to them, to feel his mother's comforting touch, but his legs wouldn't move. Fear kept him rooted in place, paralyzed by the knowledge that the world outside their home was far more dangerous than the chaos inside.

The cruel voices of the village children echoed in his mind.

"You're half-Chinese, half-Vietnamese. There's no place for you here, you Half-Breed bastard!"

Hung squeezed his eyes shut, trying to block out the taunts, but they wrapped themselves around him like chains, tightening with every passing day. His world had shrunk to one of survival—not just from the fists and kicks of the other children, but from the hateful words that seemed to pierce deeper than any blow.

His small frame, his quiet nature, and his naivety about the world outside their shack made him an easy target. The slums of Hon Gai, nestled beside Ha Long Bay in Quảng Ninh Province, were transforming into a battleground. The war between Vietnam and China had stirred long-buried tensions, and families like Hung's—caught in the middle—were viewed with suspicion and hatred.

Violence was everywhere, and bullying had become a grim reality of daily life. Fear hung over the village like a heavy cloud, suffocating and inescapable.

That morning, Hung sat quietly by the doorway, watching his mother as she carefully picked up the broken glass. Despite everything, she always tried to bring a fragile sense of beauty into their home, keeping flowers in a small vase on the table. But even that beauty was fleeting, shattered by the hatred that surrounded them. As Hung watched her, his stomach churned with helplessness. He could hear his father's voice from outside, talking about the boat again, about leaving.

Escape seemed like their only option. Yet, despite his father's determination, Hung could sense the sadness in his eyes. A deep reluctance hung in the air, like a weight no one wanted to speak of.

Hung wanted to believe that leaving would make things better. He had heard stories of faraway places, lands where people of all kinds lived together in peace.

Sometimes, late at night, he allowed himself to imagine what life would be like in such a place, free from the taunts, the violence, the fear. But hope was a dangerous thing, fragile and easily broken. Like the glass in their window, it could shatter without warning. Better to accept the misery of the present than to dream of something better, only to have those dreams crushed.

In the days that followed, Hung noticed small things disappearing around the shack—his mother's wedding ring, a few pieces of gold hidden under the floorboards.

His father was preparing for their departure, selling whatever they could spare. Hung didn't know the details, but he understood enough to know that money—or gold—was essential for their escape. Despite his father's resolve, a heaviness hung over the family, a sense that they were walking toward an uncertain future.

One afternoon, while his mother was sweeping the floor, Hung saw a man approaching from the hill outside. He was tall and thin, his gaunt face and sunken cheeks evidence of days, perhaps weeks, without enough food.

He was part-Chinese, like their family, and there was something desperate in his eyes. Hung's mother noticed him too, and she rushed to the door.

"You shouldn't be out here," she called to him, her voice laced with concern. "You don't have the strength to make it back up the hill."

The man stopped but didn't turn. His voice was weak, hoarse, barely carried by the wind. "They beat up my boy. Broke his hand. Made him steal our rice. I'm going to get it back."

Hung's mother gasped, her hands trembling as she gripped the doorframe. "They'll kill you."

The man didn't flinch. "Then so be it," he said, his voice steadier now. "But if I let them take what's ours, what kind of father am I?"

Without another word, the man turned and continued down the hill. His steps were slow, deliberate, but filled with grim determination.

Hung watched from behind the door as a group of men approached, their voices loud and slurred with drink. They were laughing, boasting about beating up a young boy. **"Did you hear the crack when I stepped on his hand?"** one of them jeered. **"Brought the rice right back to us!"**

The man stopped, his face contorted with rage. He straightened his back, his fists clenching at his sides, and marched toward the group. Hung's mother called after him, her voice rising with desperation, but her words were lost in the wind.

Lanh, the biggest of the group, was the first to notice the man approaching. He grinned, a cruel sneer spreading across his face. "What's the matter, old man? You come to take your rice back?"

The man didn't respond. Instead, he surged forward with a speed that caught them off guard. In a single, fluid motion, he drove his fist into Lanh's solar plexus. Lanh staggered backward, gasping for breath, his eyes wide with shock. Hung's breath caught in his throat as the man followed up with a sharp palm strike to Lanh's chin, sending him crumpling to the ground. For a brief moment, the man stood victorious, his chest heaving with exertion.

But the victory was short-lived. Slim, seizing the opportunity, pulled a heavy stick from his belt and brought it down on the man's head with a sickening crack. The sound echoed through the street like breaking bone, and blood splattered across the dirt. The man crumpled to the ground, motionless.

The others moved in, kicking and stomping until there was nothing left but a bloodied heap. Hung's heart pounded in his chest as he watched from the shadows. He had just witnessed a man die, and the reality of it hadn't fully sunk in. Why had the man fought? Why hadn't he run? Four young men against one sick, frail old man—it made no sense.

Hung slipped back inside the shack, his body trembling as he replayed the scene in his mind. The fear inside him had grown, tightening its grip, suffocating him. But something else stirred deep within—a question, a flicker of something he didn't fully understand.

As night fell, Hung lay on the thin mat that served as his bed, staring up at the ceiling. His mother's soft sobs echoed through the room, but Hung's thoughts were consumed by the day's events. The old man had chosen to fight, knowing it would cost him his life. Why? The fear inside Hung was overwhelming, paralyzing. How could anyone fight against that?

Yet, as he drifted into a fitful sleep, one thought lingered in his mind: **What if there was a way out? A way to fight fear, rather than be ruled by it?**

CHAPTER 2

THE HAUNTING HILLS

"The greatest glory in living lies not in never falling, but in rising every time we fall." – Nelson Mandela

Hung crouched behind a dense clump of under-growth, heart pounding in his chest. His mother's voice cut through the humid air, sharp and commanding. He didn't want to go back, didn't want to face the dread that now clung to every corner of their broken home. Reluctantly, he slipped through the narrow gap in the shack's wall, the rough corrugated metal scraping against his small frame.

As he reached the familiar corner where his younger brother, Quân, sat playing quietly, Hung tried to calm his racing heart. He crouched beside him, picking up a stick and pretending to draw patterns in the dirt. His mother entered, her sharp eyes scanning the room, suspicion flickering in her gaze. She narrowed her eyes but said nothing, leaving Hung to wonder if she had noticed his absence.

The next morning dawned with the sound of distant gunfire. Another nightmare had come to life.

The Violence Creeps Closer:

The village, once vibrant and full of life, had become a battlefield. Each day, Hung awoke with a sense of dread, as if the walls of their small shack were closing in, suffocating him. The violence, once distant, now crept closer, a beast clawing its way toward their doorstep.

Hung pressed himself into the shadows of the corner as he watched, his eyes wide, and his heart thudding painfully in his chest. From his hidden vantage point, he saw a truckload of soldiers roar into a nearby alley, kicking up dust and debris as they descended on a neighbor's home.

The rain came down in heavy sheets, turning the dirt road into thick, sucking mud, but it did nothing to deter the soldiers. They moved like a pack of wolves, tearing through the home with merciless efficiency.

A woman, drenched and shaking, stood outside, trying in vain to shield her children with trembling arms. Hung's stomach twisted. He couldn't look away. His small frame shook as he witnessed the soldiers beat the woman's husband and brother, their bodies crumpling under the relentless blows. Blood mixed with the rain, flowing like a macabre stream through the mud.

Hung's breath caught in his throat. He wanted to scream, to run, to do something, but fear held him in place. *What if it was their family next?* The image of the woman's desperate eyes, her body huddled over her children, seared itself into Hung's mind. It was a sight he would never forget.

The Desperate Departure:

That same morning, before the sky had fully brightened, Hung's father and older brother had left. The violence was escalating, and they had no choice but to flee. Hung had watched as his father gathered what little gold they had, his face etched with a grim determination.

Chaos reigned at the docks, where Hung's father and brother were immediately confronted with unimaginable brutality. Refugees packed the harbor, desperate to escape the horrors of the war. The scene was nothing short of a nightmare—a cacophony of screams, the frantic wailing of children, and the violent shoving of people who had run out of time.

Hung's father had sold nearly everything they owned to secure passage, but it wasn't enough for all of them. His heart heavy with guilt, his father had taken Hung's older brother and promised to find a way to bring the rest of them over as soon as possible. The image of their small, overcrowded boat fading into the horizon, the dark waters of the China Sea swallowing them whole, haunted Hung's dreams.

The Crushing Weight of Waiting:

For Hung and his mother, time moved slowly, every second a weight pressing down on their chests. The days stretched out like the oppressive heat that clung to the air, thick and suffocating. His mother did her best to maintain a sense of normalcy, but even Hung could see the cracks forming in her resolve.

She stood by the window for hours on end, staring at the distant hill that led to the harbor. Hung often caught her muttering prayers under her breath, her hands wringing the fabric of her worn dress. The weight of the silence grew heavier with each passing day, and the unspoken fear that his father and brother might never return gnawed at them both.

As the sun dipped below the horizon each evening, long shadows stretched across the village, transforming the landscape into something sinister. The familiar sounds of neighbors laughing or pots clattering in the streets were replaced by an eerie quiet, broken only by the occasional scream or gunshot.

Hung couldn't shake the feeling that the village itself was slowly dying, like a living thing succumbing to disease. The ghosts of the dead seemed to linger in the air, their whispers carried on the wind. He peered into the darkness, half-expecting to see the restless spirits of those who had perished, their faces twisted in pain.

The Village on the Brink:

The village was crumbling. The vibrant marketplace, once full of life, now stood deserted, its stalls overturned and looted. The few remaining families, those with Chinese heritage, huddled together in their homes, waiting for the inevitable. The soldiers—rebels, as some called them—had made it clear that anyone of mixed blood was an enemy.

Even the animals seemed to sense the approaching doom. The chickens no longer clucked with enthusiasm, and the dogs, once loud and boisterous, now skulked in the shadows, their tails tucked between their legs. The tension in the air was palpable, like the village itself was holding its breath, waiting for the final blow.

Hung's mother became more vigilant, refusing to let him or Quân out of her sight for more than a few moments. She barricaded the door every night with chairs and pieces of furniture, knowing it was futile but doing it anyway. It was the only defense they had left.

The Lull Before the Storm:

Hung's world had become a twisted blend of nightmare and reality. He often woke up drenched in sweat, unsure if the horrors he had seen were real or just the remnants of a bad dream. The line between the two had blurred beyond recognition.

In the rare quiet moments, when the village seemed to hold its breath, Hung allowed his thoughts to drift. He imagined what it would be like to escape—to leave the village behind and find a place where the sun always shone, where the air smelled of flowers instead of smoke and blood. In his dreams, his family was whole again. They were safe, far away from the terrors that now ruled their lives.

But these dreams were fleeting, always interrupted by the harsh reality that escape was not something they could afford. With each passing day, the fear of losing his father and brother grew, and the weight of waiting pressed heavier on his chest. He didn't know how much longer they could hold on.

A Mother's Resolve:

One evening, as the sun dipped below the horizon and the shadows stretched long and thin across the village, Hung's mother made a decision. She had been standing by the window for hours, her gaze fixed on the hill, waiting for a sign—any sign—that her husband and son were still alive. But no sign came.

"We're leaving tomorrow," she said quietly, her voice trembling with a mix of fear and determination. "We can't wait any longer."

Hung stared at her, wide-eyed. He had never heard his mother sound so certain, so resolute. She had always been the strong one, holding their small family together in the face of unimaginable hardship. But now, even she was breaking. He didn't know where they would go, but if his mother said they were leaving, then that's what they would do.

Facing the Unknown:

That night, as Hung lay on his thin sleeping mat, he listened to the distant sounds of chaos. The screams, the gunshots, the crackle of fires—it was the soundtrack of their lives now. But tonight, amidst the terror, there was something else. A glimmer of hope, faint but present.

Hung closed his eyes and let the sound of his mother's quiet breathing lull him to sleep. For the first time in what felt like forever, there was a sense of calm within him. He didn't know what tomorrow would bring, but they couldn't stay in the village any longer. They would face whatever dangers lay ahead—together.

CHAPTER 3

THE TIDE OF FEAR

"Fear is the mind-killer. Fear is the little death that brings total obliteration." —Frank Herbert, Dune

Countless bodies washed ashore with each tide along the rocky coast of Halong Bay. Cold, lifeless forms drifted like forgotten memories, reminders of the never-ending conflict. Even near the harbor at Hon Gai, where fishermen hauled their nets, the waves deposited their tragic cargo. Desperation gripped the villagers, who scavenged for whatever they could find—clothing, trinkets, anything to barter for food. It had become routine, this grim dance with death, a testament to the lengths they were forced to go just to survive.

Hung's mother was one of those combing the beaches. Her face was etched with lines deeper than her years, her hands rough and calloused from endless days of searching. Day after day, she returned with small scraps of wood, metal, or cloth—her only treasures. Each piece, though insignificant, was precious because it kept them alive for one more day. Yet with every item she picked up, she carried another weight—one heavier than the sea-worn debris. The fear that one day, among the dead, she might find the faces of her husband or eldest son.

Hung, confined to their tiny shack as much by his mother's orders as by necessity, grew restless. He was a boy of boundless energy, stifled by the oppressive atmosphere of their home. His younger brother, Quân, fended for himself while Hung found ways to sneak out.

The shack had become a cage, one made worse by the cruelty of the village children who taunted him whenever they saw him. Their words, sharp and venomous, cut deep: *Half-breed*, *Chink*, *Outsider*. With each taunt, Hung's spirit withered a little more.

As the days stretched into months, the absence of his father and older brother became unbearable. Silence filled their lives, the space where their presence should have been was a void that only grew darker with time. The village, already cold and hostile, now felt like a prison, with Hung and his family on the fringes, unwelcome and unwanted. The isolation was suffocating, pressing down on him like the weight of the endless sky. No matter how much he tried to shake it off, the blanket of hopelessness wrapped tighter around his small body.

A Gift of Survival:

On Hung's eighth birthday, a small event broke the monotony. His mother handed him a small pocket knife. It was a gift from his father, given before he left. The blade was chipped, its once-shiny surface dulled by years of use, but to Hung, it was more precious than gold. It had been the last thing his father had given him before he left—before everything fell apart.

Flashback:

The late afternoon sun slanted through the cracks in their small home. Hung's father, a quiet man, called him over to the corner of the room where a small wooden chest lay open. Inside, nestled among a few worn belongings, was the knife.

"Hung," his father said in his deep, steady voice, "this knife has been with me since I was your age. It's not much, but it has seen me through hard times. Now, I'm giving it to you." He paused, placing the small blade into Hung's hands. "This is a tool, not a toy. Use it wisely."

The knife felt heavy in Hung's small hands, more from the weight of responsibility than its actual mass. His father placed a firm hand on his shoulder, his grip steady, but there was something more in his eyes—a gravity that Hung couldn't yet understand. "A man must protect what is his—his family, his honor. But sometimes," his father continued, "the best way to protect is to avoid danger. This knife is a last resort, Hung, not the first."

Hung nodded solemnly, the weight of the knife mirrored by the weight of his father's words. Even then, at such a young age, he understood that this was more than just a gift. It was a duty.

Hung had carried the knife with him ever since. It was a symbol of his father's strength, a reminder of the man who had taught him how to survive. But it was also a burden. Every time Hung touched the blade, he was reminded that one day, he might have to use it.

The Alley:

One evening, after a particularly grueling day at school, Hung found himself hurrying home. His mother had sent him to the market to buy gardening tools after theirs had been stolen in the night. The market was crowded, and despite searching through the stalls, he couldn't find what he needed. Dusk had already begun to settle, casting long shadows over the street. He quickened his pace, his breath coming in short, sharp bursts as he tried to outrun the encroaching darkness.

As he approached the narrow alley leading up the hill to his village, the sun's warmth faded, leaving him alone in the growing gloom. The alley loomed before him, a dark, unwelcoming tunnel that seemed to stretch into the abyss. Hung hesitated, the familiar grip of fear tightening around his chest, squeezing his breath until it felt like he might suffocate. His pulse quickened, the shadows playing tricks on his mind, turning every pile of trash and every rusted tin into the shape of something waiting to strike.

He knew the danger. If he didn't make it home before dark, the men who prowled the streets would find him. And that was a fate far worse than the fear gnawing at him now.

His knees trembled, his hands slick with sweat, as his breath came faster. The alley, narrow and suffocating, seemed to close in, swallowing him whole. The stench of ammonia, urine, and rotting food clung to the air, choking him. He covered his mouth, fighting back the bile that threatened to rise. Each sound—footsteps, distant voices, even the wind—seemed magnified, as if the darkness itself was alive and watching him.

Tactical Training:

His father's voice echoed in his mind: *Control your fear, Hung. The greatest battles are fought not with fists or weapons, but with the mind. If you let fear take over, you've already lost the fight.*

Hung closed his eyes, trying to steady his breathing. He exhaled slowly, forcing the terror to loosen its grip. But when he opened his eyes again, the fear was still there, as real as the shadows that surrounded him.

He muttered to himself, "Nope, that didn't work." But then something shifted inside him. His father's words sank deeper. *Fear is part of you. But it doesn't have to control you. Turn fear into focus.*

With trembling hands, Hung reached into his pocket and unclipped the knife from its sheath. The cold metal pressed against his skin, oddly comforting despite its dulled blade. It wasn't much, but it was all he had.

He gripped the handle tightly, forcing his legs to move. Step by step, he entered the alley, the darkness wrapping around him like a heavy cloak. His senses sharpened as he moved, every sound and smell more vivid. His feet echoed in the alley, the only sign of life in this dead zone between the safety of the village and the lurking danger of the streets below.

A voice pierced the silence, cutting through his thoughts. "That's how I feel about you Chinks being here," someone whispered from deeper in the alley.

Hung froze, the voice chilling him more than the night air. His heart slammed in his chest, and for a moment, the world narrowed to that voice. His mouth went dry as he tried not to move, his eyes darting around the alley. Seconds later, the shadows released a figure that loomed toward him.

"Don't think this is the place you're looking for, little boy. Why don't you go home, you Half-Breed Chink?"

Instinctively, Hung began backing up, his mind racing through options. He'd been cornered. As he worked through his retreat plan, he bumped into something solid behind him. His heart skipped a beat as an older boy, hidden in the shadows, grabbed him by the head, pulling him down toward the ground.

Panic surged. Without thinking, Hung pulled the knife from his pocket and thrust it backward over his head. He felt the impact as it struck the boy behind him, though the knife was still in its sheath. His mind scrambled for control as the other boy reached for the weapon. In his panic, the older boy only grabbed the sheath, pulling it free just as Hung yanked the knife back for another thrust.

The Fight:

The blade, though chipped and rusted, sliced through flesh with surprising ease. Hung felt the warmth of blood spill over his hand as the boy released his grip, dropping to his knees with a muffled cry. One of his eyes had begun to close, a line of blood trickling from where Hung had struck. For a moment, time seemed to freeze, the reality of what he had done sinking in. He had hurt someone— seriously hurt them.

Before he could process, another figure emerged from the shadows, grabbing him by the shoulder and spinning him around. The second boy was taller and leaner, his limbs gangly but quick. A twisted grin spread across his face as he backhanded Hung across the cheek. Pain exploded in Hung's face, his cheekbone burning from the force of the strike.

Dazed, Hung would have fallen if the first boy hadn't still been gripping his clothes. As the taller boy reared back for another strike, Hung reacted. He thrust the knife forward, catching the boy in his side. The blade slid through fabric and skin with shocking ease, and the boy screamed, collapsing to his knees, clutching his side as blood spilled from the wound.

Hung's heart pounded in his ears, the sound almost drowning out the boy's cries. His legs trembled beneath him, but the adrenaline coursing through his veins forced him to act. Without thinking, he spun around, bolting past the remaining boys who had been lurking in the alley.

Their mocking smiles vanished, replaced by shock as they saw the blood on Hung's hands.

The fear that had once paralyzed him now fueled his flight. He could feel his pulse throbbing in his temples, his body screaming for rest, but he couldn't stop. Stopping meant facing a danger far worse than what he'd already encountered. He had to get home—home was safety, home was the only place left.

Aftermath:

By the time Hung reached his shack, his chest burned, and his breath came in ragged gasps. He stumbled through the doorway, his heart still pounding, sweat dripping down his face. His mother glanced at him, concern etched on her face, but he quickly turned away, hiding the bruised, swollen side of his cheek.

"The market didn't have what you wanted," he mumbled, his voice barely audible as he moved to his sleeping pad, avoiding her eyes.

His mother started to say something, her voice tinged with concern, but Hung didn't wait to hear it. He collapsed onto his pad, pulling the thin blanket over his head, shielding himself from the world outside. Beneath the cover, his body shook, not from the cold but from the fear that still clung to him like a second skin. He felt the sting of tears burn his eyes, but he fought them back, determined not to let them fall.

As the adrenaline faded, exhaustion took over, and despite the throbbing pain in his cheek and the images replaying in his mind, sleep eventually claimed him.

Reflection:

That night, Hung's dreams were a chaotic blur of shadows, blood, and echoes of the fight. He relived the moment he thrust the knife into the boy's side, the sensation of flesh giving way beneath the blade, and the sound of the boy's scream. But even more haunting was the weight of what he had done. He wasn't a child anymore—not after tonight.

Hung could hear his father's voice in his mind, distant but clear: *This knife is a last resort, not the first.* But tonight, he had used it as his first and only option. Had he failed his father? Or had he simply done what was necessary to survive?

Hung didn't have the answers, but as he lay in the darkness, he knew that the village—the world around him—demanded something different now. Innocence was a luxury he couldn't afford. Fear would always be there, pressing in on him like the tide, but now, he understood something new. Fear wasn't something to push away; it was something to wield. He could turn fear into focus, into a weapon as sharp as the knife he carried.

This was the real lesson his father had tried to teach him. *Tactical Training* wasn't just about physical survival. It was about mastering the mind. Hung would need to learn how to control his fear, how to use it to make him sharper, more aware, and more prepared for the dangers that lurked in the shadows.

As the dawn crept into their shack, Hung stirred. His body ached from the fight, and the side of his face still throbbed, but something inside him had shifted. He wasn't the same boy who had left for the market yesterday. He was someone who had faced fear—and survived.

The Next Morning:

The light of day mocked the terror of the night before. The sun filtered into the shack, casting long shadows across the floor. Hung's muscles protested as he forced himself to rise. He could hear his mother bustling around, preparing for the day, but he couldn't face her yet—not

after what had happened. He knew there would be consequences for what he had done in the alley, and sooner
or later, those consequences would catch up with him.

But for now, he had to keep moving. He had to stay
ahead of the tide of fear that threatened to sweep him
under. The knife in his pocket felt heavier than it had
before. It was no longer just a tool—it was a reminder of
the line he had crossed, a line that marked the beginning
of something new, something darker.

With each passing day, the boy who had once been
driven solely by fear began to grow into something more.

The seeds of resilience, planted by his father's
teachings and watered by the harsh experiences of his
life, were beginning to take root. Hung was learning how
to rise above the tide, how to swim against it, and how
to face the world without flinching.

Whatever the future held, Hung was determined not
to be swept away.

CHAPTER 4

THE RECKONING

"Courage is resistance to fear, mastery of fear—not the absence of fear."— Mark Twain

Hung awoke to a sharp, stinging pain spreading across his face. A dull throb radiated from his swollen cheekbone, each pulse a reminder of the violence that had exploded the night before. His eyes fluttered open, the dim light filtering through the cracks in the wooden walls of the shack offering little comfort.

Every movement felt like a battle, the soreness in his muscles protesting as he shifted, trying to find a position that didn't send waves of discomfort through his body.

He inhaled slowly, wincing as his ribs expanded under the strain. The metallic taste of blood lingered on his tongue, a sickening reminder of the previous night's chaos. The memory of it—the boy's face twisted in anger, the desperate thrust of the knife—flooded back all at once, bringing with it a nauseating sense of dread. Hung blinked, trying to clear the fog from his mind, but the weight of the night clung to him like a second skin.

He turned his head to the side, the ache in his neck intensifying. Quân lay beside him, his small body curled into a tight ball on the makeshift pad they shared, clutching a toy fashioned from sticks and feathers. The innocence in his brother's peaceful expression cut through Hung's heart like a blade. How could someone so pure live in a world this harsh? A deep, aching protectiveness stirred within him. Quân deserved better—better than a world where every day was a struggle for survival, better than this life of fear and violence.

Hung forced himself to his feet, his muscles screaming in protest with every movement. Each step felt like a test of willpower, the sharp pain in his limbs slowly subsiding into a dull, persistent ache. He limped toward the small cooking area, his hands trembling slightly as he began to prepare rice. The rhythmic stirring of the pot did little to calm the storm brewing inside him. His thoughts kept drifting back to the night before—each moment replaying in his mind, vivid and haunting.

The knife. The fight. The boy's scream.

The knife had been his last line of defense, the only thing standing between him and the world intent on crushing him. Yet now that the adrenaline had worn off, guilt gnawed at him. The boy wouldn't forget. Revenge would be inevitable. In this endless cycle of violence, was there any real escape?

As he stirred the rice, the monotonous motion of the wooden spoon in the pot became a metronome for his racing thoughts. His father's voice echoed in his mind:

"A knife is a tool, Hung, but it's your mind that wields it. Control your thoughts, and you'll control your actions."

At the time, those words had seemed so simple, almost naive. Now, in the quiet of the morning, they felt like a puzzle with missing pieces—fragments of a larger truth he had yet to fully grasp.

Hung paused, staring into the steaming pot. He was beginning to understand. His father's lessons weren't just about surviving physically—they were about navigating a world where every decision could mean life or death.

It wasn't just about the knife; it was about the mind that guided it. Strategy. Foresight. Hung had acted out of desperation the night before, without considering the consequences. Now, he was paying the price.

His father's words came back to him, clear and steady:

"A true warrior knows when to fight and when to wait."

Hung realized he hadn't just failed in the fight; he had failed in preparation. Surviving wasn't just about defending himself—it required outmaneuvering enemies before they even knew a battle had begun. The **Tactical Training (TT)** his father had tried to instill in him wasn't just for combat; it was a mindset for life.

Just after midday, as Hung was preparing rice for himself and Quân, a sudden series of crashes echoed from a few shacks down the track. His heart skipped a beat, and the cup of water he was holding slipped from his fingers, splashing onto the dirt floor. Hung froze for a moment, his pulse quickening as he raced to the window.

The sight outside confirmed his worst fears.

Two large thugs stood menacingly in the street, their faces twisted with intent. Between them was the boy he had stabbed the night before, his face swollen and bruised, his eyes locked on Hung's shack. The leader of the group—known as "Psycho" for his sadistic tendencies—had an older man by the collar, slapping him repeatedly and demanding information. Hung's stomach churned as he watched the man's trembling hand point toward their home.

Without wasting a second, Hung ducked away from the window, heart pounding in his chest. He grabbed Quân by the arm, whispering fiercely, "We have to go. Now." Quân's wide eyes filled with fear, but he nodded, trusting his older brother without question.

Hung guided him toward the small gap in the back wall, the same gap they had used many times before when danger had drawn too close. His thoughts raced as they crawled through, his body tense with fear of being spotted. If the thugs found them, no amount of strategy or tactics would save them. The knife he had hidden under his pillow wouldn't be enough this time. They needed to vanish before it was too late.

As they slipped into the shadows behind the shack, Hung crouched low, pulling Quân close. His mind raced, replaying the events of the previous night. He had defended himself, but only barely. The gaps in his knowledge were glaring—his father's lessons felt half-understood, fragmented pieces of wisdom he hadn't yet fully absorbed. He needed more than brute strength. He needed tactical skill—something to give him an edge.

A rock crashed through the window, shattering the last of their pottery. The sound pierced the air, reverberating like a gunshot. More rocks followed, each one pounding against the walls with relentless force. The barrage seemed to go on forever, a violent reminder of the danger closing in on them.

Hung's body tensed as he pulled Quân further into the shadows, shielding him with his own. Quân trembled beside him, silent but terrified. The sounds of destruction inside their home were almost too much for Hung to bear, but he forced himself to stay focused. He couldn't afford to let fear paralyze him. Not now.

Through a crack in the timber pile, Hung watched as the thugs kicked in the shack's door. The door swung open with a deafening crash, barely hanging on its hinges as Psycho and his men stormed inside. The last thug, rushing to catch up, didn't duck in time and bashed his head on the rusty door frame. Blood streamed down his face, but he only cursed, pressing a rag to his wound.

"Where the hell is the fuckin' kid? He's dead meat!" the thug yelled, rage flashing in his eyes. His words echoed in the empty shack, but the others ignored him, too focused on tearing the place apart.

Hung's heart ached as he watched them destroy what little they had. Piece by piece, their meager possessions were smashed or thrown aside. His mind raced with thoughts of what he could have done differently—how he could have avoided this. His father's words echoed again: *"A true warrior knows when to fight and when to wait."* Before, they had felt distant, abstract. Now, they resonated deeply.

This wasn't just about fighting. It was about strategy. Patience. The ability to choose the right moment.

The thugs left the shack in ruins, their rage spent. Hung waited, straining to hear if they were truly gone. Only when he was sure did he release Quân's hand and slip back through the gap. The sight that greeted him was devastating.

Everything they owned lay in shambles.

Hung moved quickly, trying to clean up before his mother returned. He pushed debris to the sides, swept up the broken pottery, and tried to make the shack look less like a battlefield. But it was hopeless—the damage was too great.

Minutes later, his mother arrived. Her face was a mixture of shock and fury, her eyes darting from the wreckage to Hung. The bruises on his face told her all she needed to know.

"I knew it!" she screamed, her voice trembling with frustration and fear. "You just won't listen! How many times do we have to move? How many times do we have to lose everything because of your fighting?!"

Before he could respond, she grabbed him by the arm and dragged him outside. In a blind rage, she tied him to the tree in front of their home and fetched the thin branch she used for sweeping. The first strike came swift and hard, a mix of anger, disappointment, and helplessness.

Hung bit back his cries, determined not to show weakness, even as the pain seared through him.

When it was over, she untied him, her anger still simmering. "Stay here," she ordered, her voice thick with emotion. "Don't move."

Hung curled up on his sleeping pad, his body aching from the beating, his mind racing with dark possibilities. He knew the boys would come back—they always did.

The thought gnawed at him, keeping him awake long after his mother had retreated to the other room. His mind replayed the night's events, over and over, searching for a way out of this endless cycle.

Quân slipped back into the shack through the secret hole, laying down beside Hung without a word. Hung didn't need to say anything. His thoughts were consumed by his father's lessons—by the idea of mastery. Mastery of the mind, the body, the spirit. He wasn't there yet. But if he wanted to survive, if he wanted to protect Quân, he would have to get there.

As night fell and Hung finally drifted into a restless sleep, the elder's words echoed in his mind: *"To master the body, one must first master the mind. But true mastery comes only when the spirit is calm, like a still pond reflecting the sky."* The lesson that once seemed so distant and abstract now resonated with new meaning.

Hung realized that if he was to survive, if he was to protect Quân and himself from the relentless threats they faced, he would need to find that inner calm—the mastery of self that would allow him to navigate this brutal world.

Dawn broke with the faint sounds of the village waking up, the distant clatter of pots and the muted conversations of those who had managed to sleep through the night. Hung stirred from his sleep, his body still aching but his mind sharper, more focused. The echoes of the elder's lesson lingered in his mind, mingling with the teachings of his father. There was a glimmer of resolve forming within him, a determination not to be broken by the horrors of his world. He would learn, adapt, and grow stronger, no matter how long it took or how painful the journey might be.

Rising slowly, wincing at the pain that flared in his bruised limbs, Hung looked over at Quân, still asleep.

His brother's peaceful expression stirred something deep within him—a fierce resolve that had been growing since the night before. He would protect Quân at all costs, but more than that, he would become the protector his father had always wanted him to be.

Hung set about quietly cleaning up the shack, his movements careful and deliberate. Each piece of broken pottery, each splintered piece of wood, was a reminder of what they had lost. But it was also a reminder of what he still had—a chance to learn, to grow, to become something more than just a scared boy hiding from the world.

As the first rays of sunlight filtered through the cracks in the walls, Hung finished his task. The shack was far from perfect, but it was cleaner, more orderly—a small step toward reclaiming some sense of normalcy. His mother would see that he was trying, that he wasn't just a troublemaker but someone who was learning, evolving.

He stepped outside, the cool morning air a welcome contrast to the stuffy interior of the shack. The village was coming to life around him, the familiar sounds and smells a strange comfort in the wake of the chaos. Hung knew that the day would bring its own challenges, but for now, there was a quiet resolve in his heart—a determination to face whatever came next with the strength and wisdom his father had tried to impart.

This reckoning was just the beginning, but Hung was ready to face it. He would master his fear, control his actions, and find the calm within the storm. For Quân, for his mother, and for himself, Hung knew he had to become something more. And with each passing day, each challenge faced and overcome, he was getting closer to becoming the person he needed to be.

Hung took one last deep breath, feeling the cool air fill his lungs, and then turned back to the shack. Quân would be waking soon, and there was still much to do. The path ahead was uncertain, filled with dangers and trials, but Hung was ready to walk it. This was his journey, his reckoning, and he would face it head-on, with the courage and determination that would one day make him more than just a survivor. He would become the master of his fate.

CHAPTER 5

SECRETS IN THE SHADOWS

"The secret of getting ahead is getting started." — Mark Twain

Hung's life felt like a never-ending storm, each gust of misfortune driving him deeper into chaos. His mother, frustrated with his constant mischief, decided a change was necessary. The solution came in the form of hard labor: working in the rice fields owned by her brother—Hung's uncle. They lived in a neighboring province for the time being, but the threat of being uprooted hovered over them like a dark cloud, always looming, ready to cast them into the unknown again.

For Hung, working in the fields was both a blessing and a curse. On one hand, it meant an escape from his mother's sharp tongue and harsher blows. Out in the fields, he had the freedom of space and a clear view of any trouble that might come his way, usually in the form of local thugs. His primary task was to care for his uncle's two water buffaloes—large, stubborn beasts that required constant attention—feeding, watering, and bathing them daily. Hung also had to guide the buffaloes from their pen to the fields, where they would laboriously drag the heavy plow through thick, clinging mud.

The work was grueling, the kind that wore down both body and spirit. The mud splattered everywhere, coating both man and beast in filth. The buffaloes seemed to enjoy the mud, using it as a natural shield against the relentless swarms of insects that plagued them from dawn until dusk. Their tails flicked in vain as flies gathered around open wounds on their thick hides. These wounds became breeding grounds for maggots, wriggling beneath their skin, adding to their misery. Each morning, the buffaloes would roll in the mud, covering themselves in a thick layer of filth that offered some relief.

For Hung, the mud was a constant assault on his senses. The stench was unbearable—a pungent mix of decay, manure, and standing water. The fields were fertilized with a blend of animal and human waste, the smell intensified by the oppressive heat. Even after washing, the stench clung to Hung's skin and hair, a reminder of the labor that consumed his days. Insects swarmed the buffaloes, and when they couldn't reach the animals, they turned their attention to Hung, biting any exposed flesh and leaving painful welts.

Then there was "The Bastard"—a buffalo as foul in temperament as he was in odor. Unlike most buffaloes, which were generally docile, this one seemed to have a personal vendetta against Hung. He would shove him with his massive head, sharp horns gleaming, or kick out whenever Hung got too close, especially when it was time to put on the harness. The creature was a menace, and Hung quickly learned to give him a wide berth whenever possible. Even calling him "The Bastard" felt like an understatement.

One sweltering afternoon, Hung led the buffaloes back from the fields, his body aching from the day's labor.

Too exhausted to walk the entire distance, he decided to hitch a ride on one of the buffaloes. Wisely avoiding The Bastard, he climbed onto the back of the other buffalo, a sluggish beast he had nicknamed "Blossom"—a name that felt ironic given her horrendous stench.

Riding on Blossom's back was no easy feat. Hung's legs strained to maintain balance, but it was far better than trudging through the mud on foot. Blossom moved at a slow, steady pace, and Hung didn't mind. The slow rhythm was a welcome respite. Blossom didn't need much guidance, and even The Bastard, for once, seemed content to follow without causing trouble.

As they walked, Hung's thoughts drifted to the daily challenges he faced. The work was back-breaking, but it was teaching him something valuable. Out in the fields, he was learning to read the buffaloes' moods, to anticipate trouble before it arrived, and to endure discomfort without complaint. This, he realized, was his version of **Knowledge Transfer (KT)**—lessons learned not in a classroom but in the harsh, unforgiving environment of the fields. The work was shaping him, teaching him to adapt, to grow stronger with each passing day.

The fields were more than just a place of labor. They were a proving ground, testing Hung's endurance and resolve daily. His growing awareness of the world and his place in it marked the beginning of his **Transforma-tional Growth (TG)**. Each day brought new hardships, but also new strength. He was no longer just a boy trying to survive—he was becoming someone who could face challenges and come out stronger on the other side.

His reflection was abruptly interrupted when he noticed another water buffalo approaching from the opposite direction. A boy, slightly older than Hung, sat astride the animal. Like Hung, he wore only shorts and a nón lá, the traditional Vietnamese farmer's hat, his skin dotted with angry red marks from insect bites.

The narrow track they were on left little room to maneuver. As they drew nearer, the boy's expression shifted from indifference to hostility. Hung felt a prickle of unease. Something about the way the boy looked at him set off alarms in his mind.

As they approached, Blossom and the other buffalo stopped, their massive bodies nearly touching. Hung and the boy were now knee to knee, with no room to avoid each other. The track was too narrow—any sudden movement, and they'd both risk falling into the ditches on either side.

The boy's eyes narrowed, his expression twisting into a sneer. "Get out of the way, Chink!" he spat, his voice dripping with venom.

Hung's pulse quickened. He had faced insults like this before, but they always sent a surge of anger and fear through him. Before he could respond, the boy grabbed a thick bamboo stick and swung it at Hung's head. The blow landed with a sickening thud, sending Hung's head snapping forward. Stars exploded in his vision, and pain surged through his skull.

Another blow came, harder than the last. Hung's vision blurred, and he struggled to remain conscious. Blood poured from the back of his head, soaking his shirt and dripping onto Blossom's back. The boy, his strength waning, dropped the stick and grabbed Hung by the neck, pulling him into a headlock. Despite the blood covering Hung's head, the boy tightened his grip, cutting off Hung's air.

Panic surged through Hung as his vision darkened. He could feel the boy's arm tightening around his throat, his breathing becoming labored. But even through the haze of pain and fear, something inside him clicked. This wasn't the first time Hung had faced danger, and it wouldn't be the last. His **Tactical Training (TT)** kicked in. He had survived countless beatings, scrapes, and skirmishes. He knew how to think fast, how to act when it mattered most.

Desperation sharpened his thoughts. He had to get out of this. His mind raced through the lessons his father had taught him—the teachings of survival, of using whatever he had to stay alive. With a burst of strength, Hung twisted his head slightly and bit down—hard—on the boy's thigh.

His teeth sank deep into the boy's flesh, driven by a primal need to survive. Hung clamped his jaws shut, then wrenched his head back, tearing through the boy's skin. The warm, metallic taste of blood filled his mouth as he spat the chunk of flesh onto the ground.

For a moment, time seemed to freeze. The boy's eyes widened in shock as he stared at his leg. Blood poured from the gash, pulsing with each heartbeat. The realization of what had happened dawned on him, and a piercing scream tore through the air.

The boy released Hung, who managed to pull himself upright on Blossom's back. The scream startled both buffaloes. Blossom bolted forward, driven by fear, and The Bastard followed, yanked along by the rope tied to his nose ring.

Hung clung to Blossom's back with all his might. Falling now would mean being trampled under The Bastard's hooves. Blossom's frantic gallop was unstoppable, and all Hung could do was hold on as she raced back toward the pen near his uncle's house.

By the time they reached the pen, Hung was barely holding on. Blossom skidded to a halt, her sides heaving from exertion. The Bastard slowed as well, snorting and pawing at the ground. Hung slid off Blossom's back, his legs trembling, his body covered in blood—some of it his own, some of it the boy's.

Hung didn't learn the boy's fate for several days, but he knew trouble was coming. The boy was the son of the headman from the next village—a fact that didn't bode well for Hung or his family. Despite his injuries, the boy had managed to stay on his buffalo long enough to get home. By the time he arrived, he was barely conscious from blood loss. His mother quickly wrapped his leg, applying a tourniquet to stop the bleeding. A doctor was summoned immediately.

The headman's family had connections—powerful ones. They knew people in the local authorities and the police. When the boy recovered enough to speak, he gave a description of Hung, conveniently omitting the part where he had instigated the attack. It didn't take long for the police to identify Hung as the assailant in what they described as an "unprovoked assault" on an older boy.

Hung, however, was lucky. The policeman assigned to handle the case was tired of the petty conflicts that constantly erupted between villagers. He had no desire to complicate matters further by arresting a young boy.

Though the headman demanded harsh punishment, the policeman had other plans.

He approached Hung's mother with a clear warning. He was fed up with the disturbances that seemed to follow Hung and his family wherever they went. Like many others in the village, he harbored a deep prejudice against "Half-Breeds" like Hung. His disdain was clear, and his message was simple: he didn't want to see Hung causing any more trouble. If Hung crossed the line again, there would be severe consequences.

Hung's uncle, already troubled by the incident, saw the danger in continuing to shelter his nephew. His family's standing in the village was at risk, and he wasn't willing to jeopardize it for Hung. He told Hung's mother in no uncertain terms that they could no longer stay. It was time to leave, once again, and return to Hon Gai, near Ha Long Bay. The brief sense of stability they had hoped for in this village was shattered.

Furious and overwhelmed, Hung's mother lashed out at him, her blows fueled by fear and frustration. The beating was as much about her own desperation as it was about punishing her son. She had hoped that working for her brother would keep Hung out of trouble, but now those hopes were in ruins. With no other options, she began gathering their few possessions, preparing for yet another move.

Hung didn't resist. The sting of his mother's blows was nothing compared to the weight of his guilt. He hadn't meant for things to escalate so violently, but he had done what he needed to survive. As the days passed and their departure loomed closer, he often thought of the boy with the bite wound. He never learned the boy's fate, but somewhere, out there, was someone with a chunk of flesh missing—a permanent reminder of their brutal encounter.

Their departure was swift, as it always seemed to be. Hung had become accustomed to leaving, never staying in one place long enough to feel truly settled. Each new village brought the same old labels: "Half-Breed," "troublemaker." The burden of his identity followed him wherever he went, casting a long shadow over his every interaction.

As they traveled back to Hon Gai, Hung stared at the horizon, his thoughts filled with uncertainty. He had believed that growing older and stronger would make things easier. But now, as he sat in the back of the bus, watching the fields pass by, he realized something important: the bigger he grew, the bigger his problems became.

The fields had taught him much. They had shown him how to endure hardship, how to anticipate danger, and how to survive. But even with all the lessons he had learned, one truth remained: survival came at a cost. And for Hung, that cost was constant movement, constant uncertainty, and the nagging sense that he would never truly belong anywhere.

CHAPTER 6

THE GAUNTLET

"It is not the strongest of the species that survive, nor the most intelligent, but the one most responsive to change."— Charles Darwin

By the age of nine, Hung had come to understand that survival meant adapting—quickly and ruthlessly—to the realities around him. School was his battlefield, a place where he fought not only for his physical safety but for a sense of belonging in a world determined to reject him. The playground was a war zone, the corridors a gauntlet, and the classroom offered no sanctuary from the prejudice that ran deep in the hearts of his peers.

As Hung stepped onto the school grounds, a familiar knot tightened in his stomach. It had been this way for over a year now, ever since *Psycho* and his gang had marked him as their daily target. They harassed him relentlessly, day in and day out, hoping to break his spirit.

But despite the bruises, the jeers, and the pain, Hung had learned to endure. Each day, he walked into the gauntlet with the quiet determination of someone who refused to be broken.

The air was thick with the tension of an impending confrontation. Psycho rarely worked alone anymore—

he had learned that one-on-one fights with Hung didn't end well for him. Hung was too quick, too cunning, to be cornered by a single person. Now, Psycho always made sure his gang was nearby, ready to swarm at the first sign of resistance.

"Hung, *Chink*," a sneering voice called from behind him. Hung tensed but kept walking, his eyes forward. He didn't need to turn around to know who it was."Why don't you piss off home?" the voice mocked. A boy with thick glasses and a smirk stepped in front of him, blocking his path."Yeah, go home, freak," another boy chimed in, their laughter cold and biting.

Hung's jaw tightened, but he didn't respond. He had learned that words only fueled their cruelty. Instead, he let the insults wash over him, hardening his resolve. Every taunt, every cruel word was another blow, but Hung had developed a way to absorb them. The pain didn't disappear—it burrowed deeper, settling in the pit of his stomach—but it no longer had the power to cripple him.

There were few in the school who didn't see Hung as an outsider. Among them were the Vietnamese twins, Tranh and Duong. To most of the students, they were as much outsiders as Hung was—odd, different, and therefore not worth knowing. But to Hung, they were something close to friends. They didn't see him as the "Half-Breed" everyone else did. Instead, they recognized him as someone trying to navigate the same hostile world they were trapped in.

The bond between Hung and the twins had been forged in violence. During their first encounter with a group of older boys—a brutal *Beat Down*—the twins had stood with Hung. Together, they fought back with a ferocity that surprised even themselves. They may have been outnumbered, but they fought like animals, refusing to be cowed by the fifth graders who thought they could rule through fear.

Since that day, the twins had been Hung's allies. Yet, he knew better than to rely on them too heavily. Some days they were around, but other days they were not, and Hung had to fend for himself. He couldn't afford to grow dependent on anyone. He had to be strong enough to survive, even when he was alone. And, more than that, he had to be strong enough to protect the few people he cared about.

There were days when Hung would show Tranh and Duong the fresh bruises from his latest encounter with Psycho's gang. The twins never said much in response, but their admiration for Hung's resilience was clear.

They respected his ability to endure, to take beating after beating and still come back the next day. They saw something in him that most people missed—something tough, something unbreakable.

One afternoon, as the three of them wandered through the fields near the village pond, Tranh unexpectedly threw a punch at Hung's arm. Without thinking, Hung dodged it and retaliated with a flurry of blows, his fists moving faster than even he had anticipated. Tranh stumbled back, stunned, clutching his chest as he gasped for breath.

"Holy crap," Duong muttered, wide-eyed. "That was fast."Tranh laughed breathlessly, rubbing his ribs. "You're getting scary, Hung. I don't think you need us anymore."

Hung gave a small, tight grin. "It's not about needing anyone. It's about survival. The more they hit me, the tougher I get." His fingers flexed, feeling the calluses that had formed from years of using his fists. His body was lean, his muscles hardened from countless fights and relentless running. He had learned to heal faster, to ignore the pain, to keep going even when his body screamed for rest.

The next day, Hung arrived at school, his senses heightened as he scanned the yard. Tranh and Duong were nowhere in sight. Instead, he saw the usual group of bullies prowling like predators, their eyes searching for their next victim. Hung's instincts kicked in, and he slipped behind a tree, observing the scene with a cold detachment that he had learned to cultivate.

It didn't take long for the bullies to zero in on their target—a small Chinese boy who had the misfortune of crossing their path. They dragged him to the ground, kicking him as he cried out in pain. Hung's fists clenched at his sides, his heart racing as he watched the scene unfold. He wanted to step in, to help, but he knew better.

Intervening would only make things worse for the boy—and for himself.

Just when it seemed the torture would never end, Mrs. Le, the fearsome dinner lady, stormed across the yard. She grabbed the bullies by their collars and dragged them off the boy without a word, hauling them toward the school building. Their laughter turned to yelps of protest as they realized they were in trouble.

Hung let out a slow breath, the tension in his chest easing. He didn't need to fight today.

Inside the headteacher's office, Mrs. Nguyen listened as Mrs. Le explained what had happened. Her face was lined with exhaustion, worn down by the constant stream of fights and complaints. After hearing the report, she made a decision.

"Enough," she said, standing and addressing the gathered students. "If you all have so much energy for fighting, then clearly you need more work to do. Get out your math books and start working on Chapters 3 through 6. You're not leaving this school until every single one of you has finished."

The students groaned in unison, dragging their feet as they made their way to the classrooms. Hung slipped into the crowd, his mind still buzzing from the violence he had witnessed.

As he passed through the doors, Tranh caught up with him, clapping a hand on his shoulder."Meet us after school, Hung. We've got something to show you," Tranh said, his grin wide.Duong nodded in agreement. "Yeah, you're gonna love this."

Hung gave a slight nod, though a sense of unease had settled in his stomach. Whatever they had planned, it wasn't likely to be good.

That afternoon, as Hung left the school, the gauntlet awaited. Older boys lined the corridor benches, their legs stretched out to trip or kick anyone who passed. It was a daily ritual, one that Hung had learned to navigate with near-perfect precision. His father's voice echoed in his mind: *"Life will throw punches at you. You can't dodge them all, but you can learn to brace for the impact."*

Hung moved with the grace of a predator, his body taut and ready to react to the slightest movement. His senses were honed, alert to every shift in the air. He had learned how to anticipate the blows, how to slip through the gauntlet with minimal damage. It was a skill, just like any other, and he had perfected it.

As he weaved through the legs and elbows, a kick landed sharply against his shin. Pain flared up his leg, but he ignored it, pushing forward. Pain was a constant companion, but it no longer had the power to slow him down. He was beyond that now.

When he finally stepped through the heavy doors of the school, the afternoon sun bathed him in warmth. For a brief moment, Hung stood still, letting the light wash over him. There was something different about today—something in the air that made him feel lighter, more determined. He couldn't quite explain it, but he knew that he was changing.

The gauntlet, the insults, the beatings—they weren't just obstacles anymore. They were shaping him, hardening him into something stronger. One day, Hung knew, he would walk through that gauntlet without fear. Not because the blows had stopped, but because they no longer mattered.

He was becoming untouchable.

CHAPTER 7

STREET LESSONS

"The streets have taught me that there's no shortcut to success—only hard-earned lessons." — Tupac Shakur

Hung had always known the world was unfair, but the streets taught him just how ruthless it could be. In this unforgiving classroom, survival wasn't just a lesson—it was an unrelenting test, and every mistake could be fatal.

Inside the cramped, stuffy classroom, Hung sat where he always did—far in the back. The Vietnamese kids, the ones with futures that didn't involve scrounging for food or dodging bullies, claimed the front seats. Behind them sat the Chinese children, already a step down on the social ladder. But Hung, a **Half-Breed**, was at the bottom. He was pushed to the farthest corner, where even the faint whispers of opportunity struggled to reach him. At nine years old, he could barely read or write, his voice just strong enough to get by, but the streets—his true school—offered a different kind of education.

Break time became his sanctuary. He was always the first out the door, darting into the dusty streets before anyone could catch him. His feet carried him to the small hill the kids called *I-Cee Hill*, where an old woman lived in a crooked, weathered hut. She worked for a wealthy family in town, stealing chunks of ice from their freezer and trans-forming them into small, crystalline treasures by mixing the ice with a sweet syrup made from crushed plants. On sweltering days, that ice was more precious than gold.

Hung was quick, both in body and mind. By now, he had learned that the streets rewarded speed and cunning. He picked up on every opportunity, especially at the dimly lit gambling den, a place where desperate men and women wasted their time and money. Hung found his niche, becoming their runner. The gamblers didn't want to leave their tables—not for cigarettes, not for booze, not even for water. So Hung filled that need, fetching whatever they wanted and marking up the price.

He was clever enough to sneak cigarettes from the local market and resell them at a premium. His clients, too engrossed in their games, paid without complaint.

He never smoked the cigarettes himself—he knew better than to waste his valuable merchandise. When Hung indulged, it was with **thuốc lào**, a powerful tobacco smoked through a bamboo pipe. The first time he tried it, the world spun, his body convulsed, and foam bubbled from his mouth as his mind faded into darkness. But like everything else on the streets, he adapted, and soon, he could handle the potent smoke. Sometimes, when the water in the pipe ran dry and none of the boys were sober enough to fetch more, they would top it off with their own piss, too far gone to care about the difference.

Running became his escape from the world, from the cruel classroom, and from his place at the bottom of the social hierarchy. His hustling barely earned him more than a few coins at a time, but in his world, that small fortune bought him moments of freedom. And sometimes, those moments came in the form of a sweet ice cube from the old lady on *I-Cee Hill*—a fleeting piece of happiness in an otherwise brutal existence.

Yet, the streets weren't just for running; they were a battleground too. Hung had seen it before—how the bigger, stronger kids took whatever they wanted, leaving the weaker ones to fend for themselves. He always kept his head down, trying to stay out of sight, but today was different.

Hung arrived at the old lady's hut, only to find that the ice had run out. One of the bigger kids, a brute with a reputation for his violent temper, spotted a smaller boy who had managed to get the last piece of ice. In an instant, the bully was on him, snatching the ice away and kicking the boy to the ground, laughing as he did it.

Hung felt that familiar twist of fear in his stomach, the same warning he always felt when trouble was near. It told him to stay quiet, to avoid the situation altogether. But this time, something new stirred within him—a deep sense of injustice. He had seen enough of the strong preying on the weak. He'd had enough.

The bully, chewing on the stolen ice, turned to face Hung, unaware of the rage building beneath his surface. Hung's mind raced, recalling the lessons he'd learned on the streets: **Tactical Training (TT)**—assess the situation, act swiftly, and use whatever you have.

Hung clenched his fists, his eyes narrowing as his body tensed. His head screamed at him to walk away, to let it go. But his feet moved on their own, carrying him forward. Before he could think twice, he stood beside the boy who was still on the ground, offering him a hand. In his other hand, Hung held a small piece of ice he had managed to buy earlier, now wrapped in cloth, turning cold and heavy.

The bully, seeing Hung approach, sneered. "What, you want some too, Half-Breed?" His fist pulled back, ready to strike, but Hung was ready.

Time slowed. Hung's mind became razor-sharp as he instinctively twisted his body, just as his father had once taught him. He shifted his weight to his back leg and, in a single, swift movement, drove his ice-filled fist into the bully's chin. The impact was brutal—the ice shattered in his hand, the cold shards slicing into his knuckles, but he didn't feel the pain. All he felt was the shockwave of force as the bully's head snapped back.

The bully staggered, his teeth clamping down on his tongue, blood spraying across the ground. The street fell into silence.

For a heartbeat, Hung thought it was over, but the bully found his balance. He spat out a mouthful of blood, fury burning in his eyes, and charged at Hung like a wild beast. Before Hung could react, the force of the bully's shoulder crashed into him, sending him sprawling to the ground. Pain exploded in his ribs as the bully's weight pressed into him. Hung gasped for breath, struggling to recover, but there was no time. A heavy kick slammed into his stomach, knocking the wind out of him and sending him rolling across the dirt.

Hung's vision blurred as his face slammed into the ground. He could taste the blood in his mouth, feel the sting of his loosening teeth. His mind screamed in panic, but amidst the chaos, a primal instinct kicked in. This wasn't over. Not yet.

As the bully grabbed the back of his neck, pulling him up to slam his face into the ground, Hung acted. He planted his hands in the dirt and pushed up with every ounce of strength left in his body. In one explosive motion, he twisted his torso, driving his elbow into the bully's throat.

The sound was sickening, a soft crunch as the bully's breath was cut short. He collapsed, clutching his throat, his scream reduced to a desperate, wheezing gasp.

Hung lay on the ground, his chest heaving as he spat out blood. His body trembled from the adrenaline still coursing through his veins. He had won—but it didn't feel like a victory. The bully lay on the ground, writhing in pain, and guilt crept into Hung's chest. He hadn't wanted to hurt him this badly, but the streets didn't care about intent.

Suddenly, the quiet was broken by the sound of people gathering. Adults, who had been nowhere moments before, rushed to the bully's side, completely ignoring Hung. He watched them for a moment, then slowly stood, his body aching with each movement. His heart pounded in his ears, but the rage that had fueled him moments ago had faded, leaving only a cold emptiness.

As Hung walked away, he knew this wasn't over. The bully would recover, and when he did, he would come looking for revenge. The streets had taught Hung how to fight and how to survive, but today they had awakened something darker inside him—something he wasn't sure he liked. That feeling, the raw violence, scared him more than the bully ever could.

His thoughts raced as he made his way back up *I-Cee Hill*, his mind torn between guilt and a strange sense of satisfaction. He had stood up for the weaker boy, but at what cost? His father's lessons echoed in his mind:

"Control your fear, Hung. Strength comes from within, not just from fighting." Hung realized that this fight had been a test, not of his strength but of his ability to stay in control. And he had failed.

By the time he reached the top of the hill, the adrenaline had worn off, leaving him feeling drained. The old lady's hut was empty, the ice long gone. He collapsed under the shade of a tree, his muscles screaming for rest.

As the sweat cooled on his skin, his mind drifted to the future. The streets weren't going to get any easier.

He had made a stand today, but tomorrow would bring new challenges, new fights, and new lessons.

Hung didn't know what the future held, but one thing was certain—he wasn't the same boy who had walked these streets yesterday. He had learned to fight, to hustle, and to survive, but more than that, he was beginning to understand the real lessons of the streets. The ruthless, unforgiving streets would keep testing him, pushing him to grow stronger, to learn faster. And though he wasn't sure he liked the person he was becoming, he knew that in this world, survival wasn't just a lesson—it was everything. The streets would not offer any reprieve. There would be no forgiveness for weakness or hesitation. Each encounter, each confrontation, pushed him further down a path that left less room for fear and more for instinct. The transformation had begun, and Hung felt it with every fight, every harsh reality he encountered.

As the afternoon shadows stretched long over the hill, Hung's mind wandered back to his father's lessons, to the fleeting moments of warmth and wisdom they'd shared before the streets had claimed him. **"Strength comes from within,"** his father's voice echoed in his memory.

Hung knew the truth in those words, but he also knew the streets had their own version of strength—one forged in pain and necessity, not just in wisdom or courage.

The bruises on his body, the sting of fresh cuts on his knuckles, and the ache deep in his chest reminded him of the cost. But they also reminded him of his victory, of the small boy he had defended, and the bully who now feared him. It was a victory laced with bitterness, a feeling Hung would come to know all too well.

For now, there was no turning back. Tomorrow, the streets would demand more from him. Tomorrow, the lessons would continue.

CHAPTER 8

BENEATH THE SURFACE

"What lies behind us and what lies before us are tiny matters compared to what lies within us." — *Ralph Waldo Emerson*

Hung awoke drenched in sweat, the oppressive heat of the early morning pressing down on him. The pain from last week's brutal fight had dulled to a faint throb, but the nerve damage from years of beatings left one side of his face partially numb—a strange blessing, he thought, as it dulled the lingering ache. But today, his mind wasn't on his injuries. Tranh and Duong had promised a surprise, one they'd kept secret until Hung was fully recovered. Today, he would find out what it was.

He dressed quickly, his hands moving automatically through the motions. The familiar silence of the shack greeted him, his mother already gone for the day. Her temper had been unbearable since the riots at the Viet Cong school, and Hung had learned to navigate her rage with careful steps. Today, though, was different. Today, his mind was clear. He repeated the words to himself like a mantra: *Today will be a beautiful day.*

His feet carried him swiftly toward the old factory near the river, where his friends were waiting. The factory loomed ahead, an imposing relic of the past. Its rusted metal surfaces were darkened by years of neglect, standing like a forgotten sentinel by the riverbank. Hung felt a sense of unease settle in his chest, but he brushed it aside. Whatever Tranh and Duong had planned, it was big, and Hung wanted to be ready.

"Hey, it's Hamburger Face!" Tranh's voice broke through his thoughts.

Hung grinned, shaking off the last of his unease. The nickname no longer stung; it was a relic of its own, like the scars he carried. Tranh and Duong had pilfered snacks on their way to the meeting—an act of survival more than mischief. Duong tossed a piece of bread at Hung, who caught it and stuffed it into his mouth, the simple act grounding him in the moment.

"So, what's the big secret?" Hung asked, his voice muffled by the bread.

Tranh flashed a grin and gestured toward the factory. "We saw them bringing something inside. Something valuable."

"Valuable how? Like gold? Or something more… dangerous?" Hung asked, his curiosity piqued despite the growing knot of anxiety in his stomach.

Duong's eyes gleamed with excitement. "The kind of stuff people hide. Which means it's worth something."

Hung raised an eyebrow, skepticism creeping into his voice. "And you think we're gonna just walk in and take it?"

"We've got a plan," Tranh said confidently.

Hung smirked. "A plan, huh? This isn't one of your 'wing it and hope for the best' ideas?"

Tranh punched Hung lightly on the arm. "Just follow us, smartass."

The three boys moved along the shoreline, sticking close to the factory's perimeter fence. The air was thick with the smell of salt and decay, mingling with the scent of damp earth as they made their way through the undergrowth. The guards patrolling the factory were lazy, more interested in their card games and cigarettes than their actual job. Still, Hung kept his eyes on them, his senses sharpening as they neared the fence.

"How exactly are we getting in?" Hung asked, his voice low. Tranh shot him a grin. "Watch and learn."

With practiced ease, they scaled the fence, slipping over the top and landing softly on the other side. The ground beneath their feet was soft and muddy, the low tide revealing a sandbar that stretched along the river's edge. Each step sank slightly into the muck, and Hung felt the familiar twist of nerves in his gut.

"Careful where you step," Tranh warned. "The sand's tricky here. One wrong move, and you'll get stuck."

Hung nodded, his mind racing with possibilities. He was constantly scanning the environment—analyzing their position, the guards' patrol routes, and the risks ahead. *Tactical thinking,* he reminded himself. *Use what you know.*

They reached a small rowboat Tranh had hidden beneath some fallen trees. The boat rocked gently as the three boys climbed in, Tranh and Duong taking the oars and guiding it toward the factory's submerged base. The river lapped against the sides of the boat, the rhythmic sound of water the only thing breaking the tense silence.

Hung's sense of unease deepened, but he masked it with a grin. "Anyone wanna tell me what this surprise is before I freak out?"

Duong chuckled, though there was a nervous edge to his voice. "You'll see soon enough."

As they approached the factory, Hung saw it: a hidden entrance, half-submerged beneath the metal structure, covered by debris and fallen trees. Rusted metal gates blocked the way, their ancient surfaces streaked with grime.

"This is it?" Hung asked, his voice low.

"Yep," Tranh said. "Let's do this."

They tied the boat to a post and slipped into the entrance one by one. The air inside was thick and stale, the smell of rust and decay clinging to their clothes. Hung's heart raced as they moved deeper into the passageway, the light from the entrance fading behind them.

The factory's underbelly was a maze of dark, forgotten spaces. Hung's skin prickled with tension, his instincts telling him something wasn't right. *Stay sharp,* he told himself. *This is about thinking ahead.*

They reached the end of the passage, where a massive iron gate stood in their way, secured with a rusted lock. Hung frowned. "And how exactly are we supposed to get through this?"

Tranh gave the gate a frustrated kick. The sound of groaning metal filled the air, and suddenly, the gate collapsed with a deafening crash. Dust and rust exploded around them, making Hung cough and wave the air in front of his face.

"Nice one," Hung said dryly.

Tranh muttered something under his breath, clearly embarrassed. "It worked, didn't it?"

Hung shook his head, but a small smile tugged at his lips. They moved past the fallen gate, their footsteps echoing through the darkened passage. The further they went, the heavier the air felt, thick with the scent of damp metal and something else—something that set Hung's nerves on edge.

In a small room off the main passage, they found what they were looking for: a stack of cloth-wrapped packets, hidden in the shadows. Hung reached out, his fingers brushing the coarse fabric. The packets were heavy, more than they should have been.

"Let's grab these and go," Hung whispered, the sense of foreboding growing stronger by the second.

Each of them grabbed two packets, and they retraced their steps back to the boat. The silence between them was thick with tension, their earlier excitement replaced by the cold realization that they had just walked into something far bigger than they had anticipated.

Once they were safely away from the factory, they beached the boat under a large tree and opened the packets. Inside were strange clay-like substances and metallic objects wrapped in cloth. Hung's stomach churned as he held one of the objects up to the light.

"What the hell is this?" Duong muttered, his voice uneasy.

Hung shook his head. "I don't know, but it feels… wrong."

The weight of the objects wasn't just physical. It felt heavy with consequences, the kind that could follow them for days, weeks—maybe even longer. Hung's mind raced with possibilities, none of them good.

"We should hide these," Hung said quietly. "Until we figure out what they are."

The others nodded, their earlier bravado completely gone. They split the packets between them, each boy taking a different route home to avoid suspicion.

Hung's mind wouldn't stop racing as he walked through the village streets, the shadows lengthening as the sun sank lower in the sky. *What if this brings more trouble than it's worth?* The question gnawed at him, tightening his chest. He had no idea what they had stumbled upon, but it felt dangerous—like the calm before a storm.

When he reached home, the shack was still empty. He quickly hid one of the packets under his sleeping pad and stashed the other along the road, just in case. The unease followed him even as he lay down, the familiar creak of the wooden bed beneath him doing little to comfort him.

His thoughts churned as he drifted off to sleep, the weight of the day pressing down on him like the heat. The shadows in the corners of his room seemed to shift and move, playing tricks on his tired eyes. In the distance, a storm began to brew, the wind rattling the shutters as lightning flashed across the sky.

Even in sleep, the unease lingered. His dreams were filled with dark corridors, the scent of rust and decay heavy in the air, and the ominous clinking of metal echoing through the silence. Somewhere, deep in his subconscious, a voice whispered warnings—warnings of the consequences yet to come.

Tomorrow, everything would change. Hung could feel it deep in his bones, a quiet inevitability. The secrets they had uncovered would not stay hidden for long. And when they surfaced, he knew he would need to be ready.

CHAPTER 9

EXPLOSIVE CONSEQUENCES

"In the midst of chaos, there is also opportunity." — Sun Tzu

Hung awoke before dawn, the events of the previous night weighing heavily on his mind. The memory of the explosives hidden in the dark factory cave replayed itself over and over like a hazy dream, each detail sharpening as he lay there in the stillness. The pride of discovery clung to him, but beneath that pride was an unsettling fear—a fear he couldn't shake. Those packs weren't just objects; they were dangerous tools capable of destruction.

Lying on the thin mat, Hung stared up at the worn ceiling of the shack, his eyes tracing the familiar cracks in the wood. Quân's soft breathing was the only sound cutting through the early morning silence. *How did we end up here?* he thought. The line they had crossed last night felt like a one-way gate—there was no going back.

Their lives had changed the moment they stumbled upon that cache of explosives. The weight of it pressed down on Hung's chest like a stone.

The air in the shack was still, but his mind was a storm of thoughts. *What now?* He had always known how to survive, how to outwit the people around him. But this was something else entirely. This was power. The kind of power that, if misused, could destroy everything. That thought sent a chill through him, breaking him from his trance.

Moving silently, Hung slipped out of bed, careful not to wake his brother. His feet barely made a sound as they touched the worn floor. Without thinking, he found himself walking to the corner of the shack, his gaze fixed on the floorboard that concealed the pack. Kneeling, he lifted the loose board with practiced ease and peered at the cloth-wrapped bundle beneath. It was still there.

Untouched. For a moment, the tension in his chest eased, but only for a moment. He quickly replaced the board and stood, running a hand through his hair.

The weight of what they had done—the weight of what they now possessed—was suffocating.

He stepped outside into the damp morning air. The village was still bathed in darkness, the sky only just beginning to lighten with the promise of a new day. The silence was almost unnatural, as though the world had paused in anticipation of what was to come. Hung's feet moved on instinct, carrying him down the familiar path toward the riverbank where his second stash was hidden beneath a pile of stones. The river's soft murmur filled the air, a sound that usually calmed him. But today, even the river couldn't soothe the growing unease inside him.

When he reached the stash, Hung crouched down and carefully checked the concealed explosives. Everything was as it should be—nothing had changed.

Still, he couldn't shake the feeling that their lives had irrevocably shifted. Standing, he glanced around, his senses heightened. The world around him felt the same, yet different, as though it held its breath in anticipation.

The village was waking when Hung returned, the sounds of daily life gradually filling the air. But for Hung, the morning passed in a blur. His mind was consumed by the explosives and what they meant. His usual distractions—pickpocketing, gambling—seemed like games compared to what they had now. This was real power, raw and untamed. His father's words echoed in his mind, cutting through the haze of thoughts: *"Power without knowledge is like a blade without a handle— dangerous and impossible to control."*

Dangerous. The word gnawed at him. They were like children playing with fire. They had stumbled upon something that could destroy them if they weren't careful.

They needed to figure out what to do, and fast. But the real question was: Could they control it?

By midday, the village was alive with the sounds of life, but Hung's focus was elsewhere. His restlessness grew with each passing hour until it became unbearable. He couldn't sit idly by, not with the weight of the explosives hanging over him like a dark cloud.

He met Tranh and Duong by the river, their usual meeting spot. The two brothers were already there, waiting with nervous anticipation. They each carried a pack, just as Hung had. There was a strange energy in the air between them—an energy that Hung both recognized and feared. It was the same energy he had felt the night before when they first stumbled upon the cache. It was the feeling of being on the edge of something dangerous.

"Why did you both bring a pack?" Hung asked, his voice low. His eyes moved between the two boys, a growing sense of unease twisting in his gut.

"We… did both bring one," Duong replied, looking at his brother for confirmation. There was a flicker of confusion in his voice, as though he hadn't really thought about it.

Hung didn't press further. Something didn't feel right, but he couldn't place it. The three of them clambered into the old rowing boat and pushed off from the shore, letting the current pull them downstream. The river was calm, its surface smooth as glass, but the tension between the boys was palpable.

They floated in silence, each of them lost in their own thoughts. Hung's gaze drifted toward the hidden factory as they passed it, the place where it had all begun. In the harsh daylight, the factory seemed even more ominous, its darkened entrance like a mouth waiting to swallow them whole. A shiver ran down Hung's spine, but he said nothing.

After about fifteen minutes, they reached a secluded cove where the river widened into the estuary. The spot was perfect for what they had in mind—hidden, quiet, far from prying eyes.

"This is far enough," Tranh said, anchoring the boat with a practiced hand. His voice was thick with anticipation.

Hung's stomach churned. "So what's the plan?" he asked, trying to keep the unease out of his voice.

Tranh's eyes gleamed with reckless excitement.

"Instead of trying to sell this stuff, let's use it." He rummaged through his pack, pulling out a piece of the gray explosive clay. Hung's heart sank as he watched Tranh press small stones into the clay, wrapping it tightly in cloth until it formed a weighted ball the size of his fist. Then, with a snap, Tranh inserted a detonator.

"That should do it," Tranh said, his voice full of pride.

Hung's breath hitched. Every instinct screamed that this was a terrible idea. "That should do what?" he asked, his voice barely above a whisper.

Tranh grinned. "Fishing bomb."

Hung stared at him, trying to wrap his mind around the concept. "A fishing bomb?" he echoed, disbelief coloring his tone.

"Yeah. You throw it in, it explodes, stuns the fish— boom! Easy haul," Tranh said, grinning wider.

Despite the growing sense of dread in his chest, Hung found himself nodding. The idea was reckless, dangerous, but there was a part of him that was curious. Curious to see what would happen. Curious to see if they could really do it.

"Well, what the hell," Duong sighed, his voice heavy with resignation. "Let's give it a try."

Tranh struck a match, the small flame flickering in the breeze. The boys exchanged nervous glances as the fuse caught, hissing like a snake as it burned toward the detonator. In one quick motion, Tranh hurled the bomb into the water.

For a moment, nothing happened. The boys leaned over the edge of the boat, tension coiling in their muscles as they waited. The seconds dragged on, and for a split second, it seemed like nothing would happen.

Then—BOOM.

The explosion rocked the boat, sending a geyser of water, fish guts, and debris into the air. The force of the blast left them drenched, their faces smeared with gore.

"Holy shit!" Tranh yelled, wiping fish innards from his face, his voice filled with a mix of excitement and disbelief.

Hung and Duong stared at him in shock before bursting into laughter. The tension that had gripped them all morning melted away, replaced by a shared sense of relief and camaraderie. They had done it. They had survived.

But as the laughter faded, so did the feeling of triumph. Hung's mind began to race again. The power they wielded was intoxicating, but it was also dangerous. A double-edged sword that could easily turn against them.

The rest of the day passed in a blur of explosions and laughter. They moved from spot to spot along the river, repeating the process over and over again. Each time, the explosions sent a thrill through them, but each time, Hung felt the unease growing in his chest. With every blast, they refined their technique, learning how to control the explosions to maximize their haul. But with every success, the danger became more apparent.

By the time the sun began to set, they had caught enough fish to feed their families for days. They paddled back upstream in silence, the earlier excitement giving way to quiet contemplation. The power they had discovered was real, but so were the consequences. They had crossed a line, and there was no going back.

After beaching the boat, the boys divided the catch. Tranh and Duong grabbed their share of fish and headed home, their voices fading as they disappeared down the path toward the village. Hung lingered, his thoughts weighing heavily on him. He stared down at the remaining fish in his hands, but his mind was elsewhere, replaying the events of the day over and over again. The explosions, the power, the recklessness—it all blurred together, creating a knot of anxiety in his chest that he couldn't untangle.

As he made his way home, Hung walked slowly, the setting sun casting long shadows across the village paths. The weight of the explosives hidden in the shack felt heavier than ever. They had discovered something powerful, something that could change everything, but the responsibility that came with it was immense. The thrill of the explosions lingered, but it was overshadowed by a growing sense of dread. What if something went wrong next time? What if they weren't so lucky?

Hung's mind raced with possibilities and dangers. He had seen power before—in the strength of the bullies who ruled the streets, in the hands of corrupt soldiers, in the violence that had shaped his world—but this was different. This power was in his hands now. *Our hands,* he corrected himself, thinking of Tranh and Duong.

When Hung finally reached his home, the village was quiet, the day giving way to night. He entered the shack silently, his thoughts still churning. His mother and Quân were already asleep, their soft breathing filling the space.

Carefully, he stashed the remaining explosives in their hiding spots, his movements deliberate and slow. Each pack felt heavier than the last, as though the weight of his choices was pressing down on him with each step.

Once the explosives were hidden, Hung changed into clean clothes, wiping the grime of the day from his skin. The cool air from the open window brushed against his face as he sat down on his mat, staring out at the darkened sky. The stars flickered faintly above, distant and cold. Hung found no comfort in their light.

That night, sleep eluded him. Every time he closed his eyes, images of the day's explosions flashed in his mind. He saw the water erupting, the boat shaking, the fish guts raining down on them. But alongside the thrill came visions of what could have gone wrong—visions of the boat being torn apart, of one of them getting caught in the blast. He imagined his mother's face, her grief if something had happened to him, to Quân.

Hung rolled over, his heart pounding in his chest. His father's words echoed louder than ever: *"Power without knowledge is dangerous."*

He understood now. The explosives were more than just a tool—they were a force, one that could easily spiral out of control if they weren't careful. They had been reckless today, caught up in the excitement of the moment, but the consequences could have been far worse.

I need to learn more, Hung thought, his resolve hardening. *If I'm going to use this power, I need to understand it. I can't afford to be reckless.*

His mind drifted back to the lessons his father had tried to teach him. The importance of knowledge, of strategy, of understanding the forces at play before acting. Hung had dismissed them before, too caught up in the immediate need to survive. But now, those lessons felt more relevant than ever.

There was so much he didn't know—so much he needed to learn if he was going to navigate the dangers ahead. The power they had stumbled upon could be their salvation, or it could be their downfall. The difference would come down to how they used it. Hung knew that if he was to protect the people he cared about—his family, his friends—he needed to be smart about it.

As he lay there, staring at the ceiling, Hung made a decision. He wasn't just going to use the explosives blindly, without understanding their full potential or their risks. He needed to learn from those who knew more than him, from the people who had mastered the kind of power he now held. His father had always talked about true masters—people who could harness power with precision, with control. Hung would seek them out. He had to. His survival, and the survival of those he cared about, depended on it.

The next morning, Hung awoke feeling more determined than ever. His path was becoming clearer, but it wouldn't be easy. He would have to tread carefully, learn quickly, and above all, avoid the pitfalls of arrogance and recklessness. The power they had wasn't just a tool for survival—it was a tool for change. But that change could swing either way, for better or for worse.

As he stepped outside into the crisp morning air, Hung took one last look at the village around him. The world hadn't changed, not yet. But inside him, something had shifted. His journey was far from over. In fact, it was only just beginning.

There were forces in play far greater than he had ever imagined, and if he was going to survive—and protect those he loved—he would need more than brute strength. He would need knowledge, wisdom, and a deeper understanding of the world around him.

As the sun rose on the horizon, casting its first light over the village, Hung's resolve hardened. He wouldn't be reckless again. He couldn't afford to be. The stakes were too high, and the power he held was far too dangerous to wield carelessly. He would learn, he would grow, and he would master the forces at his command.

His father's words echoed one last time in his mind: *"Power without knowledge is dangerous."* And Hung knew, with a certainty he hadn't felt before, that he would seek out the knowledge he needed to wield that power wisely.

    The journey ahead was uncertain, filled with danger and unknowns. But Hung wasn't afraid anymore. He was ready.

- 75 -

CHAPTER 10

THE PLAN

"Plans are nothing; planning is everything."
— Dwight D. Eisenhower

Hung's heart raced as he walked beside Tranh and Duong after school, his excitement barely contained. Each step felt heavier as the plan swirled in his mind, growing bolder with every passing day. The sun hung low in the sky, casting a warm glow over the village, but Hung's thoughts were consumed by something far more intense. The plan—this plan—could change everything.

For too long, Psycho and his gang had terrorized them, humiliating Hung and his friends. But this was no longer just about revenge. It was about reclaiming their pride, proving that they weren't weak, that they wouldn't be pushed around anymore. The humiliation burned like a fresh wound in Hung's chest, but today, that fire was fuel.

"I've been thinking," Hung said, his voice betraying a hint of excitement despite his attempt to sound casual.

Tranh, ever quick with a joke, grinned. "Careful, Hung. Thinking too much might hurt that big brain of yours."

Hung chuckled, but the intensity simmering beneath his smile was impossible to hide. The time for jokes was over. This wasn't a game anymore. His hands tightened into fists at his sides, the memory of Psycho's taunts still fresh in his mind.

"You think this is funny?" Hung shot back, his voice a little sharper than he intended. "What if I told you I have a plan—a real plan—to take down Psycho and his gang once and for all?"

Both Tranh and Duong stopped in their tracks, the teasing smirks fading from their faces as Hung's words sank in. The weight of his statement hung in the air, heavy and serious. Tranh exchanged a glance with Duong, both of them clearly intrigued.

"What kind of plan?" Duong asked, his brow furrowed in suspicion.

Hung's pulse quickened. He could feel the shift—their attention was locked on him now, waiting for his next words. The thought of Psycho's face twisting in fear sent a thrill through him.

"We don't need real explosives," Hung began, lowering his voice to a conspiratorial whisper. "Just the detonators.

We make Psycho and his gang believe we've set a bomb. They'll panic, thinking they're about to be blown to pieces."

Duong's eyes widened. "You're serious?"

Hung nodded, his confidence growing with every word.

"We'll trap them in Old Phuoc's yard. No one goes there because of the smell. It's perfect. We'll set up bamboo fencing to block their escape, light the detonators, and watch them squirm."

Tranh's expression shifted from skepticism to interest. "Bamboo fencing? Where are we going to get that?"

Hung had already thought of everything. "We'll steal it from the market stalls by the docks. If we're quick, no one will notice it's gone until it's too late."

Duong wrinkled his nose, already imagining the foul odor of Old Phuoc's yard. "That place smells like death."

"Exactly," Hung said, a sly grin spreading across his face. "The smell is bad enough, but once they think the whole place is about to explode, they won't care about the stench. They'll be too busy trying to save themselves."

The look of intrigue in Tranh and Duong's eyes told Hung everything he needed to know. They were hooked. The plan was taking on a life of its own, and the excitement buzzing in Hung's veins only intensified.

As they continued walking, Hung's mind wandered back to a memory he couldn't shake. He was eight years old, standing behind his father, too afraid to confront the older boys in the village who had teased him. His father's hand had rested on his shoulder, firm and reassuring.

Face your fears, Hung. You can't run from them forever. You stand your ground, or they'll rule your life.

Hung had never forgotten those words. They echoed in his mind now as clearly as they had that day. This plan wasn't just about Psycho. It was about facing his fear, about proving to his father—and to himself—that he could stand tall in the face of danger. This was his moment.

The next few days passed in a blur as Hung, Tranh, and Duong met in secret to fine-tune every detail of the plan. They scouted Old Phuoc's yard, enduring the overwhelming stench of manure and decay that hung in the air like a thick fog. No one in the village went near the place, and that was precisely what made it the perfect location. The yard was isolated, forgotten, and ripe for the trap they were about to set.

Hung's resolve only grew stronger with each passing day. Every stolen moment they spent planning, every whispered conversation after school, only solidified his determination. This had to be flawless—there was no room for error. Psycho would regret the day he ever crossed them.

On the night of the plan's execution, the air was heavy with anticipation. The marketplace was quiet, the stalls empty under the cover of darkness. Hung's heart pounded in his chest as they moved silently, stealing the bamboo panels from the dockside market. Each creak of wood and rustle of leaves sent a spike of adrenaline through his veins, but they worked quickly, each of them knowing that every second mattered.

Hung's muscles burned as they carried the heavy bamboo fencing to Old Phuoc's yard. His palms were sweaty, his arms trembling with the strain, but the thrill of what they were about to do kept him moving. The smell hit them the moment they arrived, the stench of rotting waste and manure so strong it was almost suffocating. Hung gagged, but he pushed through it, focusing on the task at hand.

They worked in silence, setting up the bamboo panels around the perimeter of the yard. Hung crouched near the manure pile, his hands digging into the filth as he placed the detonator. The cold, wet muck clung to his skin, but he forced himself to keep working. This was it. The final piece of the plan.

His father's words echoed in his mind once more. **Face your fears. Stand your ground.**

By the time they were done, Hung's nerves were frayed, his hands trembling from the cold and the weight of what they were about to do. But there was no turning back now. They were committed.

The next morning, as the first light of dawn crept through the window of his family's small home, Hung lay awake, staring at the thatched roof above him. His mind raced with anticipation, excitement, and fear. Today was the day. Everything they had planned, everything they had worked for, was about to come to fruition.

When he met Tranh and Duong later that day, there was no joking, no lighthearted banter. The air between them was thick with tension, their expressions serious as they went over the plan one last time.

"We have to be fast," Hung said, his voice steady despite the storm of nerves inside him. "Once Psycho and his gang are inside, we block the exits and light the fuse. Two minutes—that's all we'll need."

Tranh and Duong nodded, their faces set with determination. They knew what was at stake. If anything went wrong, they would be the ones trapped.

That evening, as the sun began to set, Hung's thoughts drifted into a vivid vision of what was to come. In his mind, he was already standing in Old Phuoc's yard, hidden behind a pile of rotting wood and bamboo. He could see Tranh and Duong leading Psycho and his gang toward the yard. Every step they took brought them closer to the trap.

His fingers trembled in his vision as he held the fuse, ready to light it. He could already picture the moment Psycho would realize he was caught—the fear in his eyes, the panic in his gang as they scrambled for an escape that wasn't there. The stench of decay and manure filled the yard in his mind, but Psycho and his gang wouldn't notice until it was too late. The trap would close, and they would be caged.

The vision played out in his head, over and over, so vividly that his heart pounded as if it were already happening. He could feel the tension rising, the weight of what was about to unfold pressing on his chest.
But it was just a vision—for now.

The next day would bring reality crashing down.

CHAPTER 11

THE EXPLOSION

*"Chaos is inherent in all compounded things.
Strive on with diligence." — Buddha*

The sun dipped low, casting a golden light that bathed the village in a surreal calm. Tranh and Duong sprinted along the dusty path, hearts pounding in their chests, each step heavy with the burden of their plan. The fear of Psycho and his gang had long been a distant threat, but now they were an imminent force, closing in like wolves hunting their prey.

As they reached the edge of the jungle, the twins darted into the underbrush, disappearing as though they had become one with the wild. The earthy scent of damp leaves and soil filled the air, thick with tension. Tranh's fingers tightened around the hilt of his knife, the cold metal steadying him. He crouched low, every muscle coiled and ready to spring.

Duong scanned their surroundings, his pulse quickening with each rustle in the bushes. The jungle, once their sanctuary, now felt fragile. Any sound could betray them. Each crack of a twig seemed louder, more ominous, as they crouched in silence, listening for signs of their pursuers.

Then came the sound they dreaded—the crunch of boots on the path.

Psycho's voice cut through the stillness, harsh and sharp. "Spread out! Find those rats!"

The gang moved swiftly, spreading through the village. Some headed toward the muck heap, their faces twisted in disgust at the overpowering stench. Others ventured dangerously close to the jungle's edge, their eyes scanning the underbrush. Psycho lingered, fists clenched, his rage fixated on the muck heap, unaware of the trap that lay in wait.

Hidden in the shadows, Tranh and Duong exchanged a glance, their breathing steady but their hearts hammering.

This was it—the moment their plan would unfold. Every detail, every step, was as Hung had envisioned.

Suddenly, the quiet was shattered by a thunderous crash. Fence panels rigged to fall slammed down across the path, sending splinters flying. One of Psycho's thugs let out a cry as the heavy wood pinned him to the ground.

His face hit the muck-streaked dirt with a sickening thud, his screams muffled by the filth.

But Psycho didn't flinch. His eyes remained locked on the heap, his rage blinding him to the chaos around him.

He stepped closer, ignoring the trapped gang member and the splintered panels. His world narrowed to the muck pile before him, the focal point of his fury.

Hung crouched low behind Old Phuoc's house, his back pressed against the rough wood. His fingers trembled as he flicked the Zip lighter, the small flame flickering unsteadily. The fuse lay before him, hissing faintly as it waited to ignite. **Is it too short?** The thought gnawed at him. **What if it doesn't work? What if everything falls apart?**

His father's voice echoed in his mind, calm and steady:

"This is Tactical Training. Act when it counts—no sooner, no later."

Hung took a deep breath, the familiar mantra centering him. His father had always taught him that the calmest mind prevailed in chaos. He struck the lighter again, this time with certainty, and touched the flame to the fuse.

The fuse sparked to life, hissing as it burned. Seconds stretched into eternity as Hung pressed deeper into the shadows, his pulse thrumming in his ears. **Stay calm. Everything is in place.**

Then—**BOOM.**

The explosion ripped through the stillness, a deafening roar that sent muck and debris flying in every direction. Psycho's gang was caught in the blast, their screams drowned out by the thunderous noise. Brown and yellow streaks of filth shot through the air, coating them in layers of sewage and muck.

Psycho, standing too close to the heap, was thrown back by the force. He landed in the mud, his face twisted in horror and disgust as filth covered him from head to toe. His gang, flailing in the muck, slipped and fell, their limbs tangled in the mess as they gasped and choked on the stench.

Hung watched from his hiding place, breathless. **It worked.** His heart raced with adrenaline, disbelief mingling with the rush of success. He had done it—he had pulled off the plan, and it had worked better than he ever imagined.

For a moment, a wild laugh bubbled up from deep inside him, uncontrollable. He wasn't laughing at their suffering; he was laughing at the overwhelming relief. **Control.** For the first time, Hung felt the power of true control over his circumstances.

"**Transformational Growth,**" he whispered to himself, the words taking on new meaning. This wasn't just revenge—it was proof. Proof that he could change his world, that he could take everything his father had taught him and make it real.

From the shadows of the jungle, Tranh and Duong emerged, their faces glowing with the thrill of victory. They could hardly believe their eyes—Psycho's gang, once feared by all, now lay floundering in filth, reduced to a laughingstock.

"I can't believe it worked," Duong whispered, his voice trembling with disbelief.

"We're geniuses!" Tranh chuckled, clapping his brother on the back. They turned and headed toward the marketplace, their steps lighter, the tension of the past weeks melting away with each footfall.

Villagers gathered near Old Phuoc's yard, watching the spectacle unfold. Laughter erupted from the crowd as they pointed and jeered at the sight of Psycho and his gang, covered in muck. Even Old Phuoc, though furious at the mess, couldn't hide his smirk. The once-feared gang had been humiliated in front of the entire village.

But Hung remained hidden, a quiet satisfaction settling over him. **This was the event that changes everything**, he thought. His victory wasn't just a prank—it was a personal triumph. He had taken the lessons of the **KT3 System** and turned them into something tangible. For the first time, he felt the weight of control, the thrill of bending his world to his will.

The morning after the explosion, the village buzzed with excitement. Hung stood on the edge of the marketplace, watching the villagers retell the story of Psycho's humiliation. Each version of the tale grew more exaggerated, the explosion becoming a legend in its own right.

"They looked like pigs rolling in the mud!" a villager shouted, his words met with uproarious laughter.

Hung smiled, but the satisfaction from the night before had dulled, replaced by a quiet unease. Psycho's reign of terror was over for now, but something had shifted inside him. **Is this what my father meant by transformation?** he wondered. The power he felt was intoxicating, but it carried a sharp edge, like a blade that could cut both ways.

He turned away from the marketplace and walked toward the river, the weight of his thoughts heavy on his shoulders. The water shimmered in the early morning light, its surface rippling in the breeze. Hung stared at his reflection, distorted by the gentle current. **Who am I becoming?**

The sound of rustling leaves pulled him from his thoughts. He turned to see Tranh and Duong approaching, their faces still bright with triumph.

"You should've heard the villagers this morning," Duong said, grinning. "They'll be talking about that explosion for years."

Tranh nodded. "Psycho's already left. He couldn't handle the shame."

Hung smiled, but his mind was elsewhere. **Psycho may be gone, but there will always be another.** His father's voice echoed in his mind: **"You win one battle, but the war never ends."**

"What's next?" Hung asked quietly, his gaze fixed on the river.

The twins exchanged a glance, confusion flickering across their faces. "Next?" Tranh repeated. "We won, Hung. What else is there?"

Hung's eyes lingered on the water, watching as the ripples distorted his reflection. **What else?** His father's lessons had always been clear—there was always another battle, another challenge. And now, for the first time, he understood that the victory was just the beginning.

"Next time," Hung said softly, more to himself than to the others, "we'll be ready."

He turned from the river and walked back toward the village, where the sounds of laughter still echoed in the distance. But for Hung, the victory was just a stepping stone. The journey was far from over.

CHAPTER 12

RUSH TO CHAOS

*"In the rush to chaos, clarity is your
only weapon." — Master Wong*

Hung's feet dragged beneath him as he made his way up the familiar hill toward the village, the weight of the sack on his shoulder a minor burden compared to the heaviness in his heart. Just as he neared the crest, a sound split the air—sharp, deafening, unnatural. His breath caught in his throat, and for a second, time itself seemed to freeze. Then, as if the earth had been torn apart, the ground beneath him shook violently, knocking him off balance. A thick cloud of debris shot into the sky, dark and ominous, spreading outward like the wings of an angry god.

"OH SHIT!" The words burst from his lips before he even had time to process the magnitude of what had just happened. His body moved instinctively. The sack fell to the ground as his legs took off beneath him, his feet barely touching the ground as he sprinted toward the source of the explosion. His quadriceps burned with every step, but he pushed harder, faster. Fear fueled him now, propelling him forward. The closer he got, the more his mind raced with terrifying possibilities. His heart hammered in his chest, each beat faster than the last as dread sank into the pit of his stomach.

It wasn't just the explosion itself that sent chills down his spine—it was the realization that crept into his mind with slow, horrifying certainty: **this was his fault.**

As Hung reached the edge of the blast site, his breath caught in his throat. It was worse—far worse—than anything he could have imagined. Debris was strewn everywhere. Shattered metal from shacks that had once stood firm was now embedded in the ground, while wood splinters littered the scene like deadly confetti. People rushed in every direction, their screams tearing through the air. The thick smell of burning wood and melted metal filled his nostrils, but beneath it, a more insidious scent clung to the air—**burnt flesh.**

His stomach churned, threatening to heave, but he pushed the nausea aside. He had to see it. He had to see what he had done.

Hung tried to move through the chaos, but the villagers surged around him in a blind frenzy, bumping into him from all sides. He stumbled, his foot catching on something solid. He fell hard, his face slamming into the dirt. A sharp pain shot through his ribs as he gasped for breath, spitting out grit. When he turned to see what had tripped him, the blood drained from his face.

A severed arm, charred and twisted, lay inches from his hand. Its fingers were still curled around a half-burnt cigarette. Hung recoiled, bile rising in his throat. He turned to the side and vomited, the acidic taste of it burning his throat. He wiped his mouth with the back of his hand, his body trembling violently. **This was his fault.**

The thought pounded in his head, echoing louder and louder as he forced himself to stand. His legs felt weak, but he had to keep moving. He had to see the extent of the damage.

The crowd parted for a moment, and that was when he saw it. The scene that would be etched into his mind for the rest of his life.

Lying on the ground, barely recognizable, was Butch—the large boy who had joined them the night before. Hung's heart nearly stopped at the sight. Butch's face was a grotesque mask of blistered, charred flesh, the skin peeling away in places to reveal the muscle beneath.

His skull was partially exposed where his hair and flesh had been seared clean off. His chest was a nightmare of melted fabric fused to his skin, and his ribs—glistening and broken—were visible through the torn flesh. One arm was a mangled stump, the other gone entirely.

People crowded around him, their hands shaking as they attempted to stop the blood flow, but the injuries were far too severe. Hung knew—**Butch was already dead**. It was only a matter of time before the body caught up with that reality.

Hung's legs buckled. He stumbled backward, his breath coming in shallow gasps. The world around him blurred as panic overtook him, and the sound of blood rushing in his ears drowned out the screams of the villagers. He had to get away—he had to **run**.

Without thinking, Hung turned and fled. The scene of devastation played over and over in his mind, like a film stuck on repeat. Butch's charred face, the severed arm, the acrid smell of burning—it was all **his fault**.

His feet carried him back to the shack, his breath ragged, his body drenched in cold sweat. Once inside, he tore through his belongings, tossing clothes and tools aside until he found what he was looking for: a pack of explosives. His heart dropped. One was missing.

Butch. He must have stolen it.

Hung's mind reeled as the truth hit him like a physical blow. **Butch had detonated the explosives.** But it was Hung who had brought them into the village. It was Hung who had failed to foresee the danger. His knees hit the ground as he scrambled toward the pile of rocks where he had hidden the second pack. His hands shook as he clawed at the stones, heaving them aside until the pack came into view. The detonators were still intact, but the relief was short-lived.

He sank back, his heart pounding against his chest. If Butch had detonated the entire pack, the explosion would have been large enough to destroy the entire village. The severed limbs, the shattered buildings—they were only a fraction of the destruction that could have been.

Hung's hands trembled as he replaced the stones. His mind raced with the weight of it all.

"Damn it, Butch!" Hung cursed, though deep down, he knew the truth. Butch might have been the one to set the explosion, but Hung had set it all in motion. He had failed to act with caution, and now people were dead.

Butch was dead.

Hung rushed back to the shack, his thoughts spiraling as his guilt crashed over him like a wave. His mind replayed every decision he had made, every opportunity he had missed to prevent this from happening. But no amount of thinking could undo the damage.

The stench of burnt flesh clung to his clothes and skin, refusing to let go. Even as he tried to calm himself, his heart raced with the memory of Butch's charred body. The image was burned into his mind, searing through his thoughts with every heartbeat.

Just as he reached his room, his mother's voice cut through the silence like a blade. "That boy is dead because of you!" Her voice shook with fury, and it sent a chill down Hung's spine.

His mother stormed into the room, her face twisted with anger. She grabbed his arm with a force that took his breath away and dragged him outside, away from Quân's sleeping form. Without a word, she reached for a bamboo cane. Her eyes blazed as she raised it high and brought it down on him.

The cane struck with brutal precision. Each blow landed harder than the last, searing his skin, but Hung gritted his teeth. He refused to cry out. He knew he deserved this. **He had brought this upon himself**.

Each strike felt like penance. Each one a small price to pay for the life that had been lost. The pain in his body barely registered compared to the anguish in his heart. His mother's face was a mask of exhaustion and grief by the time she finished, her chest heaving with ragged breaths.

She collapsed into a chair in the kitchen, her body shaking as she sobbed into her hands. Hung watched her for a moment, his body battered, his mind consumed by guilt. Then, with slow, deliberate movements, he gathered a few belongings into a small bag.

He knew he couldn't stay. The village would come for him. By morning, the shock would wear off, and they would be seeking justice. As much as it broke him to leave his mother and brother, Hung knew that staying would only bring them more suffering.

Hung moved silently, slipping into the shadows as he made his way to the pile of rocks. His hand hovered over the second pack of detonators. He hesitated for a moment, his mind racing. But this was the only thing of value he had left. He grabbed it, knowing full well it was a dangerous tool, but also his only bargaining chip.

As he left the village, his mother's words echoed in his mind. "That boy is dead because of you!" Each repetition was a knife twisting deeper into his heart.

Hung moved toward the harbor, keeping to the darkest shadows. His heart beat loudly in his chest, a drum signaling his impending exile. The night pressed in around him, cold and unforgiving. When he reached the abandoned hut by the pier, he slipped inside, collapsing on the cold, hard floor. The darkness was suffocating, wrapping around him like a blanket of guilt.

He curled up, his knees pulled tightly to his chest, but no matter how tightly he tried to close himself off, sleep refused to come. The demons in his stomach twisted and churned, eating away at him. The weight of his actions felt like a crushing force, pressing down on his chest until it was hard to breathe.

He was alone. Utterly and completely alone.

The night felt endless as Hung lay on the cold floor, his mind racing through the day's events, replaying them in gruesome detail. The weight of the detonators by his side was a constant reminder of his mistake—one he couldn't escape, no matter how far he ran. His body trembled, not from the cold, but from the unrelenting guilt that consumed him.

He had destroyed everything. **Butch was dead.** The boy's charred face lingered in his mind, a haunting image that clawed at his insides. His mother's furious words echoed endlessly, each syllable driving deeper into his heart: *That boy is dead because of you.*

Hung pressed his palms to his eyes, trying to block out the images, the voices, the overwhelming sense of failure. But nothing helped. He felt as though the darkness had swallowed him whole, trapping him in a void where guilt and regret were his only companions.

Time passed, but Hung couldn't tell how long he lay there, tormented by his thoughts. His body was exhausted, yet sleep eluded him. Each breath felt like a laborious task, as though the air itself was thick with the weight of his sins. The walls of the hut closed in on him, suffocating him with their silence.

CHAPTER 13

LITTLE FISH

"You cannot swim for new horizons until you have courage to lose sight of the shore."— *William Faulkner*

Hung stirred from a restless sleep, his body aching from exhaustion, every muscle protesting the effort. He squinted against the light filtering through the bamboo walls of an unfamiliar hut. His surroundings were unfamiliar—alien to him. Where am I? The events leading up to this moment swam in his foggy mind, his memories blending with the sharp pain that throbbed through his head.

A soft voice broke through his thoughts, the sound of a young boy. "Who is it, Dad?" the boy asked, his voice delicate as a whisper of wind.

There was a pause, then a calm reply. "I don't know, son. It looks like a strange kind of fish."

Hung's heart quickened. His mind jolted awake, his instincts sharpening. Fish? He winced as the throb in his head intensified. The aching in his body felt like he'd been dragged through harsh terrain. He touched his forehead, feeling the rough scabs left by his mother's beatings. The memory sent a cold shiver down his spine, but hunger gnawed at him even more.

The crackle of a fire and the sizzling sound of food reached his ears, followed by the mouthwatering smell of frying fish. His stomach churned, twisting with hunger. Instinctively, Hung tried to sit up, but his muscles were too weak. His hands trembled as he rubbed his eyes, willing his body to cooperate.

"A stomach that loud must be starving," came a voice from across the room, firm but not unkind.

Hung opened his eyes again, squinting against the light. A man stood by a small bamboo counter, calmly frying fish in a battered metal pan over an indoor fire pit. His back was turned, and his movements were slow, deliberate, and methodical, as though he had all the time in the world.

Fear clawed at Hung's insides. He needed to move, to do something—anything. He scrambled to his feet, but his legs were unsteady, his body betraying him. His eyes landed on fish scraps scattered on the floor, and without thinking, he knelt and began gathering them into a basket.

His hands shook, and the basket slipped from his grasp, spilling the contents onto the floor again. Hung froze, his heart pounding, waiting for harsh words or punishment.

But none came. The man continued to cook, his calm demeanor unbroken.

Hung's breath steadied, but only slightly. He quickly picked up the scraps again, trying to be as quiet as possible, afraid to draw attention. His stomach growled loudly, echoing in the small room, but the man said nothing, showing no sign of displeasure. He simply finished his task, moving with an efficiency that Hung couldn't understand but admired.

When the meal was ready, the man carried four plates outside to a small bamboo table. A girl, perhaps a year or two younger than Hung, followed him closely, her dark hair tousled and wild. Her wide eyes fixed on Hung for a moment, curiosity dancing in them, but she said nothing.

The man paused at the doorway and glanced at the girl. "Get another stool," he instructed softly. She nodded and obediently picked up a stool from near the door, carrying it outside. The man followed her, setting the plates down on the table.

Hung shrank back into the shadows, watching the scene unfold with cautious eyes. The man returned with the girl and the boy, the three of them moving with quiet grace. They sat at the table, the children patiently waiting, their behavior disciplined, almost like a ritual.

There was no shouting, no impatience—just calm, order, and a silence that unnerved Hung.

The man turned toward Hung. "Come and sit, Little Fish," he said. "We'll talk later."

Hung's breath hitched in his throat. The food smelled so good, but fear and uncertainty rooted him to the spot.

Why would this man invite him to the table? What did he want? His stomach twisted with hunger, but his fear of the unknown held him back. Still, there was no hostility in the man's voice—only patience.

Unable to resist the pull of his hunger, Hung found himself inching toward the table, his movements slow and hesitant. He sat on the empty stool, keeping his head low, trying to make himself as small as possible. The man didn't scold or reprimand him; instead, he simply nodded, as though Hung's presence was expected.

As they began to eat, Hung's eyes darted around the table. The food was simple but smelled incredible. The hut itself was sparse but sturdy. Bamboo walls lined with neatly arranged tools, a fire pit, and basic furnishings filled the space. Despite the simplicity, the space felt lived-in, warm, and safe. Hung ate cautiously, trying to savor each bite without drawing attention to himself.

His eyes drifted back to the man. He was not as frail as Hung had first thought. Scars covered his lean arms, and tattoos marked his skin—symbols that hinted at a past full of stories Hung couldn't even begin to imagine.

The man carried a quiet strength, one that made Hung feel both secure and on edge.

As they ate in silence, Hung's mind drifted back to the village, to the violence, the beatings, the chaos. This place—so calm, so ordered—was the opposite of everything he had known. He didn't understand how such a place could exist. Where was the noise? The harshness? How could strength come from anything other than brutality?

Hung finished eating last, taking his time, unsure of what would happen next. When the man finally excused the children, they quietly cleared their plates and retreated back inside. Hung began to stand, ready to follow, but the man raised a hand, signaling him to stay.

"Not you, Little Fish," the man said softly.

Hung's heart raced again, his muscles tense. He didn't want to be left alone with this stranger. Every instinct told him to run, to flee, but he had nowhere to go. Reluctantly, he sat back down, his hands trembling slightly in his lap.

"Where are you from, Little Fish?" the man asked, his tone gentle but probing.

Hung stared at his hands, unsure of how to answer.

His throat tightened, his mind flashing back to the village, to the fear and the violence. He didn't want to think about it—didn't want to speak it into existence.

The man waited, his gaze steady. After a moment, he said, "Let's start with something simpler. A name, perhaps? Unless you'd prefer I keep calling you Little Fish."

Hung swallowed hard, forcing the words out.

"My name… My name is Hung." His voice was barely a whisper, but he cleared his throat and tried again. "I'm Hung."

The man smiled slightly, nodding. "Well met, Hung. I'm Chien. This is my store and my home. The boy and girl you saw are my children—Kim and Sen. You've been here for a few days, recovering from your injuries. I've fed you, so I imagine you're feeling a bit stronger now."

Hung nodded slowly. The dull ache in his body had subsided, and the hunger no longer gnawed at him. He hadn't realized how much better he felt until now.

Chien stood and pointed toward the road. "About a mile down that road is a well. There are two buckets by the door. Bring back water from the well, and when you return, come in through the back door. There will be a hammock waiting for you."

Without another word, Chien turned and walked back inside, leaving Hung alone once again.

Hung stared down the road, a sense of dread creeping up his spine. His mind flashed back to his mother, to the beatings, to the villagers. What awaited him if he ever returned? The well seemed like the lesser of two evils.

With a resigned sigh, Hung muttered, "I guess that settles it, then."

He bent down to pick up the buckets, his muscles protesting with each movement. The road stretched endlessly ahead of him, the sun beating down with relentless heat. Each step felt like a battle, the weight of the buckets growing heavier with every passing moment. Sweat dripped from his brow, his breath coming in labored gasps.

Reflection:

As Hung trudged down the road, his thoughts wandered back to Chien. The man's calm, deliberate movements—his discipline—stood in stark contrast to everything Hung had known in his village. Chaos had ruled his life, but here, in this strange place, everything had a purpose, a rhythm. Hung found himself mimicking Chien's steady pace, trying to keep his breaths even, his movements deliberate. Was this what true strength looked like? Not brute force, but control? Hung didn't fully understand it yet, but he knew there was something here—something he needed to learn.

"Daddy, do you think he'll come back?" Sen asked, watching Hung from the doorway.

"I don't know, Sen," Chien replied, his tone thoughtful.

"He's strong-willed, but he's not centered. That can be dangerous."

Kim, who had been silent beside his sister, nodded. "I hope he makes it."

Chien smiled slightly, nodding. "Me too, son. Me too."

Hung's thoughts were interrupted by the sound of his own labored breathing. The well was still far away, but something inside him—something small but fierce—kept him moving. He straightened his back, wiped the sweat from his brow, and took another step. Then another.

Each step brought him closer to the well. Closer to something new.

CHAPTER 14

SHADOWS OF THE PAST

"We are products of our past, but we don't have to be prisoners of it." — Rick Warren

Hung's breath came in ragged gasps, each inhale a battle against the fatigue clawing at his body. His bare feet scraped against the dry dirt road, each step heavier than the last. The buckets hanging from the makeshift yoke across his shoulders swung precariously, their empty metal clang echoing in the silence. Ahead of him, the road stretched into the twilight, a shadowy path lit only by the fading sun.

His muscles screamed for relief, but he refused to stop. Stopping was not an option. Chien had given him this task, and Hung would see it through. His legs, burning with the strain of each step, urged him to collapse, but his mind kept him moving forward. He could not afford failure—not now, not ever.

The buckets at his sides felt like anchors pulling him into the earth. Hung paused for a moment, wiping the dust from his brow, and glanced up at the sky. The deepening indigo of the evening was peppered with the first stars. A gust of cool wind blew through, momentarily soothing the fire in his veins, only to kick up more dust, stinging his eyes.

Frustration boiled up inside him. The well was still a distant silhouette, barely visible in the dying light. How could he carry the buckets back, full of water, when even empty they felt like boulders tied to his back? He kicked one of the buckets in a fit of rage, the impact sending a sharp pain through his bare toes. He cursed under his breath, feeling the throbbing in his foot, and limped forward to retrieve the bucket. The physical pain was nothing compared to the mounting fury at his own weakness.

The anger festered in his chest. "Why did Chien set this impossible task?" he muttered to himself. "How am I supposed to make it back?" But deep down, he knew the answer. This wasn't about fetching water—it was about proving something, to Chien, and to himself.

With renewed determination, Hung pushed forward. Each step felt like it could be his last, but the well grew closer, its crooked frame rising against the night sky.

His throat burned from thirst, and his lips were cracked and dry. His body was beginning to betray him—he had stopped sweating, an ominous sign that dehydration had already begun to take hold.

When he finally reached the well, he collapsed to his knees, letting the buckets clatter to the ground. He looked down into its dark depths, seeing the faint shimmer of water far below. Slowly, with trembling hands, he lowered the rope into the well, the rough cord scraping his palms raw. When the bucket touched the water, he heaved it up with what little strength he had left.

The water sloshed over the side as he pulled it up. Without hesitation, he tipped it over his head, letting the icy liquid cascade down his neck and back. The cold water jolted him awake, cutting through the fog of exhaustion clouding his mind. He gasped at the shock of it, but the feeling was pure relief. He grabbed the bucket and drank deeply, gulping down the water until he could drink no more. The burning in his throat eased, and his strength began to return.

Hung wiped his mouth, leaning heavily against the well. His muscles still ached, and his body was heavy with fatigue, but his mind was sharper now. The stars above twinkled down at him, as if urging him on. He glanced up at the sky, a smile tugging at the corners of his mouth.

"All right," he whispered to the night. "Let's get this done."

Hung scanned the area, looking for something to help him carry the buckets. His eyes fell on a sturdy branch lying nearby. He grabbed it, snapping off the smaller twigs and threading it through the handles of the buckets. With a grunt of effort, he hoisted the makeshift yoke onto his shoulders, feeling the weight of the water settle on his body like a physical manifestation of his burden. It was crushing, but he embraced it. He felt like a small water buffalo, strong and determined, ready to carry the load despite the odds.

He took the first step, the yoke biting into his shoulders.

The weight of the buckets made his legs tremble, but he forced them forward. Each step was a victory over the pain, and he focused on one step at a time, refusing to think about how far he still had to go.

As the road stretched out before him, dark and winding, Hung's thoughts began to drift. His mind replayed the endless beatings from his past, the hunger that gnawed at his belly, the cruel words that echoed in his head. He had endured so much already—how was this any different? But for the first time, he felt like he was on the edge of something greater. This was a test of his will, a battle against himself, and he was determined not to lose.

Chien's words echoed in his mind: *"The body is just a vessel, Hung. It's the mind that carries you through. When the body fails, the mind must take over."* This was more than just a task—it was an opportunity to prove to himself that he could overcome the limits of his body, that his mind could carry him forward when his strength faltered. This was **Tactical Training (TT)**, and Hung was learning how to master it.

Suddenly, a rustling in the bushes beside the road jolted him out of his thoughts. His body tensed, his heart pounding in his chest. Was it an animal? Or something worse? His mind raced through possibilities, each more terrifying than the last. He couldn't afford to stop now—not when he was so close.

He pressed forward, his eyes scanning the darkness, every nerve on edge. The rustling grew louder, and fear clawed at his gut. His pulse quickened, and his grip tightened on the branch, the buckets feeling even heavier.

For a brief moment, he was certain that something was going to leap out of the bushes and drag him back to the hell he had escaped.

Then, with a burst of movement, a small rabbit darted across the road, disappearing into the underbrush on the other side. Hung let out a shaky breath, relief flooding his body. His muscles relaxed, but the tension remained.

Even the smallest things could unnerve him in this state of exhaustion and fear. He shook his head, pushing the thoughts away. He had to stay focused. He was almost there.

The lights of Chien's shop finally appeared on the horizon, a distant flicker of hope in the darkness. Hung's legs screamed in protest with every step, but he kept moving, his mind willing his body to continue. He couldn't fail now—not when he was so close.

Inside the shop, Chien stood by the window, watching the path. He had been waiting for Hung, knowing the boy would return, but still, a part of him wondered if he had pushed the boy too far. Hung's determination reminded him of his own youth, and he couldn't help but feel a sense of pride in the boy's struggle.

"Aahh, you silly old man," Chien muttered to himself, a small smile on his lips. "You've done it again."

Finally, Hung emerged from the shadows, the buckets balanced on his shoulders. His body was battered, and his steps faltered, but he had made it. Chien's smile deepened, and he nodded in approval.

"Very good, Little Fish," Chien whispered to himself. "Very good."

Hung stumbled up to the shop, barely able to lift his feet. He set the buckets down with a soft thud and collapsed beside them, his body giving out the moment the burden was lifted. Chien stepped out of the shop, his expression one of quiet pride.

"You've done well," Chien said, his voice filled with warmth and approval. "Come inside."

Hung followed him into the shop, his legs trembling beneath him. The warmth and familiar smell of the hut embraced him, offering a stark contrast to the cold night outside. In the back, a small hammock waited for him, along with a plate of bread and a cup of water. The sight of the food made his stomach growl, and he realized just how ravenous he still was.

He sat down beside the hammock, tearing into the bread with shaky hands. Chien watched him, his sharp eyes studying the boy. He saw the exhaustion etched into Hung's face, but also the fire in his eyes. Hung had passed the test, not just by completing the task, but by proving to himself that he could endure. This was a test of will, and Hung had come through it stronger.

Hung finished his meal and carefully placed the empty plate and cup to the side. With a sigh of relief, he climbed into the hammock, nearly flipping it over in the process. Once he found his balance, he sank into the fabric and closed his eyes. Within moments, sleep overtook him, pulling him into a deep, dreamless rest.

In the corner of the shop, Chien watched the boy sleep, his lips curving into a small smile. *"This one's got something special,"* he thought to himself. *"He just doesn't know it yet."*

CHAPTER 15

BETWEEN FEAR AND HOPE

"Hope is being able to see that there is light despite all of the darkness." — Desmond Tutu

Hung awoke to the faint sound of giggling and the soft rustle of movement. The morning sun was already heating the air, its thick, humid presence settling over the day like a suffocating blanket. Beads of sweat dotted his brow as he tried to sit up, every muscle in his body protesting the movement. His legs wobbled beneath him, threatening to collapse. He reached for the ceiling, stretching his arms wide in a futile attempt to ease the tension gripping his shoulders and calves, but a sharp spasm shot through his back, and he crumpled to the floor with a low, pained groan.

"You've pushed your body too far," came Chien's calm, steady voice from nearby. He knelt beside Hung, a figure of quiet authority amidst the chaos of Hung's pain.

"Your muscles are rebelling because you haven't taken in enough water. Hydration is essential for recovery."

Chien handed him a small cup of water. Hung's shaking hands barely managed to grasp it as he brought the cup to his lips. He drank quickly, the cool liquid soothing his dry throat. With every swallow, the tension in his muscles seemed to ease slightly, though the ache lingered, a reminder of yesterday's grueling work.

"When someone offers you something," Chien said, his voice firm but not unkind, "acknowledge it with gratitude.

Manners are the foundation of respect, and respect is what keeps chaos at bay."

The gentle reprimand stung. Hung bowed his head and returned the cup with a quiet, "Thank you, sir."

Chien's expression softened, but there was still an air of expectation in his gaze. "You've shown resilience and determination. These are important qualities, but they must be balanced with discipline."

"Thank you, sir," Hung repeated, though this time the weight of Chien's words pressed down on him, mingling with the soreness in his body.

"There's food for you." Chien gestured toward a small table where a simple meal awaited. "Eat, regain your strength, and we'll talk after."

Despite his exhaustion, the smell of food drew Hung forward. He sat at the table and ate, each bite a small reprieve from the soreness that wracked his limbs. As he ate, Chien sat beside him in silence, his presence both comforting and unnerving. Unlike the harsh gazes Hung had grown accustomed to, Chien's watchful eyes seemed to be searching for something deeper within him—something Hung wasn't sure he could provide.

Once the meal was finished, Sen appeared to clear the plate. She gave Hung a shy smile before hurrying away, her cheeks pink. Hung's gaze lingered on her retreating form, a strange flicker stirring in his chest, though he quickly pushed the sensation aside when Chien turned his attention back to him.

"Where do you live, Hung?" Chien asked, his tone direct but not harsh.

Hung hesitated, his eyes dropping to the floor. "I have no home, sir," he replied, his voice barely a whisper.

Chien's eyes sharpened. "Look at me when you speak," he said, his voice gentle yet firm. "Manners make the man."

Hung forced himself to meet Chien's gaze, the weight of the older man's scrutiny making his heart race. "I have no home," he repeated, this time with more strength behind the words.

Chien nodded slowly, as if weighing the truth of Hung's statement. "And how old are you?"

"I don't know, sir," Hung said, his voice low. "It was never something I needed to know."

Chien's gaze became thoughtful. "Not knowing where you come from makes it harder to know where you're going. Understanding your past is important if you want to shape your future."

Hung felt a flicker of shame. How could he know such things when all he had ever done was survive?

"I'd estimate you're about nine years old," Chien continued after a moment, "which means you were born around 1971 or 1972."

He stood and disappeared into his shop, returning moments later with a small tray holding two slender needles and a bottle of black liquid. Hung's stomach tightened with both curiosity and anxiety as he watched Chien tie the needles together with a fine thread.

"Pass me that bottle," Chien said, pointing to a nearby shelf. Hung complied, his hands trembling slightly as he handed over the small vial of ink.

Chien rolled up his sleeves, revealing arms covered in intricate tattoos. The markings wound their way up his forearms, each one telling stories of battles fought, hardships endured, and wisdom gained. Hung stared, mesmerized by the swirling lines and patterns.

"These tattoos," Chien said, noticing Hung's gaze, "are not just for decoration. They are reminders—each one a marker of lessons learned and challenges faced."

Hung's eyes traced the designs, every stroke and shade seemingly alive. The thought of having his own story etched into his skin filled him with a mix of fear and anticipation. His thoughts wandered to the battles he had survived, the pain he had endured—would these experiences one day be immortalized on his body?

Chien's voice interrupted his thoughts. "These marks represent the hardships I've overcome and the philosophies I've embraced. They're a testament to survival and growth. Someday, you may choose to tell your story in a similar way."

Hung swallowed hard, his mouth suddenly dry. The weight of Chien's words pressed down on him, mingling with the physical ache that still gripped his body. He wanted to ask more, to understand the meaning behind each mark, but something held him back. Instead, he simply nodded.

"Off the path you walked earlier is a small pond," Chien continued, his voice practical again. "Go wash. Clean your body and return."

Hung hurried down the path, eager to wash away the grime that clung to his skin. The pond was secluded, surrounded by thick foliage that hummed with life. He stripped off his filthy clothes and stepped into the cool water, welcoming the sting as it hit the cuts and bruises scattered across his body. Each washcloth stroke was a reminder of the pain he'd endured, but also of the strength he'd gained. As he scrubbed, his thoughts returned to Chien's tattoos—the idea of marking his body with symbols of his journey lingered in his mind, both terrifying and tempting.

When he returned to Chien's shop, the older man was waiting for him. The tray of needles and ink sat on the table, ready. Chien gestured for Hung to sit.

"This is an important moment," Chien said, preparing the needles with steady hands. "Today marks the beginning of your new life."

Hung's heart pounded in his chest as he took a seat. The significance of the moment pressed down on him, thick and heavy.

"I will give you your first mark," Chien continued. "A symbol of your first birthday—a reminder of the new beginning you're about to embark on."

Hung clenched his fists to stop them from trembling. The room felt smaller, the air thick with the weight of what was about to happen. He bit down on a small stick Chien offered as the first jab of the needle pierced his skin. The pain was immediate and sharp, searing through his hand with each strike of the needle. Hung's eyes watered, but he kept still, determined not to cry out. The ink mixed with his blood as Chien worked, and Hung's breaths came in shallow gasps, each one laced with pain.

When Chien finally finished, he bandaged Hung's hand with care. "You are no longer a Little Fish," Chien said, his voice soft but satisfied. "You are becoming a Dogfish—a small Shark. Something tougher."

Hung stared at his bandaged hand, the pain still throbbing beneath the wrapping, but there was something else, too—a strange sense of pride. The pain had been real, but it had given him something far greater.

Reflection:

In the days that followed, Chien asked Hung countless questions about his past—how he had survived, the battles he had fought, and the things he had seen. Each story Hung told became another chapter in his life, and Chien marked each one with ink, spreading the tattoos from Hung's fingers to his forearms, and eventually across his chest.

After one particularly painful session, Hung looked down at the fresh ink on his arm and saw the words **"Kiếp Nghèo Ôm Hận"** etched into his skin.

"'Poor fortune breeds hatred,'" Chien explained quietly. "When someone has suffered enough, their heart can become dark. But I will show you another way."

Hung stared at the words, feeling the weight of their meaning settle deep inside him. Chien's voice grounded him, pulling him back to the present. There was another path, one that wasn't driven by anger and bitterness.

As the weeks passed, Hung's skills grew under Chien's guidance. He learned how to handle a knife with precision, how to butcher meat with respect, and how to navigate life's challenges with a sharper mind. Chien wasn't just a mentor—he was a father figure, someone who believed in Hung when he didn't believe in himself.

Each new tattoo wasn't just a marker of his struggles, but a testament to the strength he had gained. The ink on his skin told a story of transformation, a story of a boy who was no longer defined by his pain but by the power he had found within it.

At night, as Hung lay in bed, his body sore from the day's work, he found himself filled with an unfamiliar sensation—hope. Life with Chien was difficult, but it was also rewarding. For the first time, Hung felt like he was on a path that led somewhere beyond mere survival.

And so, with each passing day, Hung's story continued to unfold, not just in the ink on his skin but in the growing strength and resilience that Chien nurtured within him. His journey was far from over, but for the first time, Hung felt as though he was walking toward something meaningful—a future filled with purpose.

CHAPTER 16

THE SMUGGLER'S TALE

"The brave man is not he who does not feel afraid, but he who conquers that fear."— Nelson Mandela

Hung woke with a quiet determination the next morning, the early light filtering through the cracks in Chien's hut. His body stirred with a sense of purpose, the lessons of the previous days echoing in his mind. Beneath his calm exterior simmered a blend of excitement and anxiety, a recognition of the challenges that lay ahead.

The morning routine was familiar, almost ritualistic.

Each movement around the small table—the soft clinking of bowls, the rhythmic shuffle of feet—spoke of years of disciplined practice. Despite the quietness of the meal, there was an energy in the air, a shared understanding that today was not just another day.

After breakfast, Chien rose from his seat. His presence commanded attention even before he spoke, his voice steady and firm as he outlined the day's plans. "We prepare the boat today. Supplies are running low, and we need to head back to sea."

Hung's pulse quickened at the mention of the boat. He had been waiting for this—a chance to prove himself on the sea that had both terrified and intrigued him. As Chien assigned tasks, Hung felt a swell of pride when his name was called. "Hung, you're with me. We'll gather supplies and ready the boat."

The air outside was crisp and cool, the tang of salt carried on the wind from the nearby sea. Hung fell into step beside Chien, his mind racing with unspoken questions. As they walked toward the harbor, the rhythm of their footsteps filled the silence, until Chien finally spoke, his voice softened with reflection.

"I've asked much of you lately," Chien began, his tone more thoughtful now. "It's only right that you know more about the man you're following."

Hung glanced at Chien, curiosity flickering in his eyes. He had always sensed that there was more to Chien's past, but the older man rarely spoke of it. Now, he listened intently, eager to learn about the man who had become his mentor.

"Many years ago," Chien continued, his voice heavy with memories, "my life was very different. I lived in South Vietnam during the war. The very boat we'll sail today— 'High Tides'—was once my lifeline. I used it to smuggle supplies and weapons up the coast to the soldiers fighting against the Americans."

Hung's imagination leapt to life, picturing a younger Chien navigating dangerous waters, evading enemy ships, and risking his life to deliver vital supplies. The weight of Chien's words settled over him like a blanket of respect and awe. This man had seen more danger and hardship than Hung could comprehend.

"I infiltrated enemy strongholds, gathered intelligence, and brought it back to the Resistance," Chien said, his voice steady but filled with the echoes of past struggles.

"Every mission required careful planning and quick thinking. The sea was dangerous, but it was often the least of my concerns."

As they reached the harbor, Hung's eyes widened at the sight of the boat. There, resting in the water, was the "High Tides"—a traditional Vietnamese junk, its wooden hull worn and weathered by years of hard use. The name, painted along the side, was faded but still legible, a testament to the boat's endurance and the strength of the man who owned it.

Hung stepped closer, the smell of saltwater filling his lungs. He ran his fingers along the boat's rough surface, feeling the grooves and scars etched into its wood. Every mark told a story—of storms weathered, battles fought, and survival earned.

For the next several days, Hung and Chien worked side by side, preparing the boat for the journey ahead.

They cleaned, patched, and loaded supplies, their hands moving in a rhythm born of necessity and experience. Hung watched closely as Chien worked, his movements deliberate and reverent, as though the boat were an old friend.

One evening, as the sun dipped below the horizon, casting the sky in shades of orange and red, Chien spoke again, his voice thoughtful. "This boat," he said, patting the hull, "she's been through more than most people can imagine. Storms, wars, everything. But she still sails on."

Hung nodded, understanding the unspoken message in Chien's words. The boat was a symbol, much like its owner—strong, resilient, and unbroken by the trials it had faced. In the weathered wood, Hung saw a reflection of his own life, battered by hardship but still moving forward.

The next morning, Chien assigned Hung the task of securing several crates on the deck. It was a simple task, one that Hung had watched Chien do many times before.

With confidence, he set to work, looping the ropes around the crates and pulling them tight, mimicking the knots he had seen Chien tie.

As the sun rose higher, casting shimmering light over the water, Hung allowed himself a moment of satisfaction.

The knots were tight, the crates secure. But as the hours passed, the sea began to change. The calm morning gave way to choppy waves, and the boat rocked beneath them with increasing intensity.

Hung stood on the deck, his muscles tense as he watched the horizon shift and tilt. Suddenly, one of the crates broke free, sliding dangerously close to the edge. Without thinking, Hung lunged forward, his fingers grasping the rough wood just in time to stop it from falling into the sea.

His heart pounded in his chest, the adrenaline surging through him as he struggled to pull the crate back to safety. Chien was at his side in an instant, his hands steady as they worked together to secure the crate once more. When the task was done, Chien turned to Hung, his expression calm but serious.

"Do you know why the crate came loose?" Chien asked, his voice low but firm.

Hung swallowed, shame washing over him. "I tied the knots wrong," he admitted, lowering his head.

Chien nodded. "Partly. But it's more than that. You didn't consider the environment—the movement of the water, the force of the waves. It's not just about tying knots, Hung. It's about understanding the forces around you and preparing for them."

Hung stood silent, absorbing Chien's words. It wasn't just a lesson in knot-tying; it was a lesson in foresight, in thinking ahead. It was Tactical Training at its core—understanding the environment, anticipating the challenges, and preparing for them.

"Let's try again," Chien said, handing Hung the rope. "This time, I'll show you how to tie a knot that will hold, no matter what."

Hung nodded, his determination renewed. As they worked together, he felt the tension in his shoulders ease.

Each knot he tied felt like a small victory, a step toward mastering not just the task but the mindset Chien was teaching him.

As the evening drew near and the boat rocked gently in the fading light, Hung sat with Chien, the day's lessons still fresh in his mind. He hesitated, then spoke the question that had been lingering in his thoughts for days.

"Sir," Hung began, "why don't you punish me when I make mistakes?"

Chien turned to him, his eyes reflecting the last rays of sunlight. "That's a good question, Hung," he said, a small smile tugging at the corners of his mouth. "It shows that you're thinking."

He paused before continuing, choosing his words carefully. "There are different ways to teach. Some people believe in punishment because they think it enforces obedience. But obedience born of fear is weak. Someone can come along and offer kindness, and that fear will crumble. What I believe in is trust. If I punish you every time you make a mistake, you might do what I say, but you won't trust me. And without trust, there's no loyalty."

Hung nodded slowly, the weight of Chien's words sinking in. It was a way of thinking he had never considered before, one that valued growth over control, understanding over fear. In Chien's teachings, Hung saw not just a path to becoming stronger, but to becoming wiser.

As the night settled over them, the stars twinkling above, Hung lay on his mat, replaying the day's events in his mind. Chien had taught him more than just how to tie knots or secure crates—he had taught him how to think, how to prepare, how to approach challenges with a calm mind and a steady hand.

And as the gentle sounds of the sea lulled him to sleep, Hung knew that he was on a journey, much like the "High Tides"—weathered, but still sailing forward, with purpose and determination.

CHAPTER 17

THE TEST OF COURAGE

*"Courage is not the absence of fear, but rather
the judgment that something else is more
important than fear." — Ambrose Redmoon*

Hung woke with a heaviness in his chest, a pressure
that matched the tension in the air around him. It
was a feeling like static, buzzing invisibly, making
the familiar sounds of Chien's home—the clatter of dishes,
the shuffle of footsteps—feel distant. Today was not like
any other day. Today was the test.

Stay focused. Follow the plan exactly, Chien's voice
echoed in his mind.

Hung's heart pounded, matching the nervous energy
coursing through him. His thoughts spun, racing ahead
to the mission, replaying Chien's instructions over and
over. The simplicity of the plan was deceptive. Today
wasn't just a test of his physical abilities. It was about
courage—his ability to face overwhelming fear and still
act. Every lesson Chien had imparted would be tested
today, and the thought made Hung's stomach churn.

At breakfast, the air between them was thick with
unspoken tension. Chien, usually calm and composed,

seemed distant, his eyes unfocused. Hung ate mechanically, the food tasteless as his mind continued to run through every step of the plan. His hands trembled slightly, but he gripped the table, steadying himself. *I can do this,* he repeated silently, clinging to the thought like a lifeline.

When the meal was done, Chien placed a small, flat bag on the table between them. The bag appeared ordinary, but its weight seemed disproportionate to its size, as if it carried more than just the object inside.

"Strap this under your shirt," Chien instructed, his voice calm but firm. "Remember, Hung, this mission is dangerous, but if you follow my instructions, everything will go smoothly."

Hung nodded, though his hands shook as he fastened the bag around his waist. The physical weight pressed against his skin, but the emotional burden—the responsibility—felt heavier. This mission wasn't just a test of his skills; it was a test of his trust in himself and in everything Chien had taught him.

They stepped outside, the bustling marketplace already alive with the sounds of vendors and shoppers. The noise was a familiar cacophony, but to Hung, it was little more than a distant hum. His focus had narrowed to the mission ahead. Each step felt like it carried the weight of the world, the tension coiling tighter in his chest.

Chien walked beside him, his low voice cutting through the marketplace's noise. "Remember, Hung, the item we're retrieving is important, but the real goal is to ensure the thief is caught and brought to justice. You must let him catch you."

The thought of letting himself be caught made Hung's stomach twist, fear curling around his insides. The idea of facing the thief's rage, of what might happen if things went wrong, sent a shiver down his spine. But he nodded, trusting Chien implicitly. This was **Tactical Training (TT)** in action—every move was calculated, every choice deliberate.

The vibrant colors and sounds of the market gradually faded as they entered a narrow alley. Shadows pressed in, and the air grew colder, heavier. Hung's senses sharpened, his pulse quickening as the tension in his muscles grew. They were nearing the house. The weight of the bag against his skin seemed to intensify with every step.

The house loomed at the end of the alley, its darkened windows like hollow eyes watching them approach. Chien gestured toward a small window on the side of the house, just large enough for Hung to squeeze through.

Hung hoisted himself up and slipped through the window, landing quietly on the other side. The stench hit him immediately—sweat, stale food, and something sour. He gagged but forced the nausea down, focusing on the task at hand. His skin crawled as he crept through the cluttered room, his senses on high alert.

The rhythmic sound of snoring filled the air, and Hung's pulse quickened. The thief—the pigment—was just beyond the next doorway. Every muscle in his body tensed as he crept closer, peering into the dimly lit room.

There he was.

The pigment, a massive figure, sprawled across the bed. His breath came in labored snores, his face hidden in shadow. Hung's eyes darted to the small blue cloth on the table beside the bed. *That's it.*

His hands trembled as he reached for the cloth, carefully lifting it and slipping it into his satchel. Relief washed over him for a brief moment. *I've done it.*

But as he turned to leave, his foot clipped a metal cup on the floor. The clang echoed through the room like a gunshot.

The pigment's eyes snapped open.

In an instant, the man was on his feet, his massive frame looming over Hung. "THIEF!" he roared, his voice shaking the walls. Before Hung could react, the pigment lunged, his hand clamping down on Hung's shoulder with bone-crushing force.

Hung tried to twist away, but the pigment's grip was like iron. Pain exploded in his side as the man's fist slammed into him, knocking the breath from his lungs.

Hung staggered, gasping for air, but the pigment wasn't finished. Another blow—a boot to his leg—sent him crashing to the ground, his knee twisting beneath him.

A scream tore from Hung's throat as white-hot pain shot through his body. The room spun, his vision blurring from the shock. The pigment loomed above him, his fist raised for another strike.

But before the blow could land, the door burst open.

Two police officers stormed in, their shouts filling the room. "Stop right there!" one of them barked as they wrestled the pigment away from Hung.

Hung lay gasping on the floor, his leg burning with agony. His knee throbbed, each attempt to move sending fresh waves of pain through him. The officer who had pulled the pigment off him glanced down with a sneer.

"Street rats like you always find trouble," the officer muttered, roughly yanking Hung to his feet.

Hung's leg buckled beneath him, the pain nearly blinding. He cried out, clutching his knee, but even through the pain, he held the satchel tight against his chest. *I did it,* he thought, his grip tightening. *I followed the plan.*

The cool night air hit his face as they stepped outside, but it did little to ease the throbbing in his leg. Nhât rushed to his side as soon as he saw them, his face pale with worry.

"Hung! What happened?" Nhât's voice was tight with concern as he moved to support Hung, wrapping an arm around his waist.

"The pigment… he kicked me," Hung rasped, his voice barely audible over the pain.

Nhât tightened his grip, guiding Hung down the alley.

Each step was agony, and by the time they reached the meeting point where Chien waited, Hung's entire body felt like it was on fire. When Chien saw them approach, his eyes darkened, his calm composure cracking for just a moment before he regained control.

Chien moved quickly, kneeling beside Hung to examine his injured leg. "What happened?" His voice was calm but laced with tension.

"The pigment kicked me hard in the leg," Hung managed through gritted teeth, his knee throbbing as Chien's fingers gently probed the swollen area.

Chien frowned, his brow furrowing as he inspected the injury. "We need to get you back," he said, his tone decisive. "Your leg needs rest."

With Chien and Nhât supporting him, Hung limped painfully back to the hut. Every step felt like knives stabbing into his leg, but despite the pain, a sense of pride swelled in his chest. He had done it. He had followed the plan.

When they finally reached the hut, Hung could barely keep his eyes open. Exhaustion tugged at him, the weight of the night's events crashing down. Chien and Nhât lowered him onto a mat, and Chien quickly set to work tending to his injuries.

The cooling salve Chien applied to his knee brought momentary relief, but the pain still throbbed in the background, a constant reminder of the beating he had endured. Hung lay there, his thoughts swirling as his body gave in to the exhaustion. Despite everything—the pain, the fear—he had passed the test.

"You did well," Chien murmured as he worked. "Rest now, Little Dragon. You've earned it."

Hung nodded weakly, his eyes fluttering shut. His body felt heavy, but in his chest, there was a strange lightness—a sense of accomplishment. He had faced fear, endured pain, and succeeded.

As he drifted into unconsciousness, Hung clung to that thought. The pain would pass, but the lesson of courage—the strength to act in the face of fear—would remain.

CHAPTER 18

THE HEALING BEGINS

*"The wound is the place where the
Light enters you." — Rumi*

Hung stumbled into the dimly lit hut, each step a searing reminder of the battle he'd just survived. Pain clawed at his body, sharp and relentless, making every movement a test of endurance. His leg felt as if it had been torn apart, the muscles screaming for relief. His ribs ached, the aftermath of the brutal strikes he had endured. But despite the agony etched into every fiber of his being, his expression remained composed.

He would not falter—not in front of Nhât, not in front of Chien. His mind was clear on that one principle: he could not show weakness.

Nhât moved quickly to Hung's side, his brow furrowed with worry. The sight of Hung's injuries was worse than he had imagined. Deep purple bruises spread across his ribs, and the shredded remains of his shirt clung to him, matted with dried blood and sweat. Even as Hung fought to stand upright, his body betrayed him, shaking under the weight of his injuries. His eyes, though, remained steady, carrying a quiet determination that seemed out of place in the battered figure before them.

Chien, ever the pillar of calm, placed a firm hand on Hung's shoulder, guiding him toward the wooden table in the center of the room. The familiar market sounds outside the hut—vendors haggling, children playing—seemed like a distant memory, far removed from the harsh reality unfolding within. Hung's breathing was labored, every breath a reminder of how fragile his body had become after the attack.

As they reached the table, Hung felt his legs begin to buckle, but Chien's hand kept him grounded. Nhât stood back, uncertain, his gaze locked on his friend.

The silence between them was heavy, filled with the unspoken fear that perhaps Hung had reached his limit this time. But Hung would not allow himself to crumble. He couldn't afford to.

Chien moved with swift precision, cutting away the remnants of Hung's shirt. The cool air hit his skin, a welcome relief from the suffocating heat. His ribs were swollen and bruised, the deep purple discoloration stretching across his side. His leg was worse. The swelling had already begun, and the unnatural angle of his shin told them all what Chien feared—a break. Still, Chien's hands were steady, his expression unreadable as he retrieved his tools from a small chest in the corner.

Nhât hovered nearby, torn between horror and helplessness as Chien worked. There was something almost sacred in the way Chien moved, his practiced hands mixing herbs and powders with deliberate care.

The grinding of the mortar and pestle filled the room, an odd sense of comfort in its rhythm, contrasting sharply with the pain that rippled through Hung's body.

Hung's mind drifted, the pain in his leg and ribs competing for his attention, but his thoughts wandered further, back to the alley where everything had gone wrong. The alley—he'd been so sure he could handle them, so certain his training had prepared him. But the weight of his enemies had been too much, and the moment his leg gave out, it was over. The thought gnawed at him, biting deep into his pride.

How did I let this happen? he wondered, his jaw clenched against the pain. *I should have been stronger. I should have fought harder.*

The exhaustion pulled at him, dragging him further from the present. His eyes fluttered shut as he recalled the moment he'd collapsed, the sharp twist of his leg, the panic in Nhât's eyes. His body had betrayed him, and it stung more than any bruise or break.

A pungent scent jolted Hung back to the present. Chien stood over him, a small cup of steaming liquid in hand. The bitter, herbal smell filled his senses, making his stomach turn.

"Drink this," Chien said, pressing the cup into his hands.

Hung hesitated for a moment, his gaze locking with Chien's. The look in Chien's eyes was steady, reassuring.

Without a word, Hung lifted the cup to his lips, wincing as the liquid burned its way down his throat. The taste was bitter, and the warmth was almost unbearable, but he forced it down, knowing there was no other choice.

The heat settled in his chest, but the sharp pain in his ribs intensified. A violent coughing fit overtook him, each hack sending shockwaves of pain through his torso. He gasped for air, his vision blurring as the world tilted dangerously.

Nhât rushed forward, his voice distant, muffled by the pounding in Hung's head. He felt the room spinning, the pain becoming overwhelming, and for a moment, he feared he might lose consciousness.

Chien's hands moved quickly, applying a cool ointment to Hung's bruised ribs. The relief was instant, the cooling sensation easing some of the tightness in his chest. Hung let out a shaky breath, his body relaxing slightly under Chien's touch.

But the relief was fleeting.

As Chien turned his attention to Hung's leg, the pain surged back with a vengeance. The swelling had worsened, the deep purple bruising spreading from his knee to his ankle. Chien frowned as he gently probed the area, his fingers careful but firm.

"This is bad," Chien murmured, more to himself than to anyone else. He reached for a bandage and began wrapping Hung's leg tightly, forming a makeshift splint.

Hung gritted his teeth, his hands clenched into fists as the splint was secured. The pressure was unbearable, but he held his breath, refusing to cry out. His mind was a storm of thoughts and memories, but above all, one thought persisted: *I have to be stronger.*

Nightmare:

Hung's mind spiraled as the pain began to fade, giving way to the exhaustion that clung to him like a shadow.

His eyelids drooped, and before he could stop it, his thoughts carried him back to the nightmare that had haunted him for days.

He was back in the village, running through the streets as flames licked the buildings. The sky was black with smoke, and the ground was littered with debris and bodies. His feet caught on something, and he stumbled, falling face-first into the dirt. When he looked up, his heart stopped.

Butch lay in front of him, his body twisted and broken, the flesh charred and unrecognizable. Hung scrambled to his feet, reaching for his friend, but Butch's eyes were empty, staring up at the sky with a pain that Hung could never erase.

"No! Butch!" Hung's voice tore through the nightmare, his body thrashing against the memory. He reached out, but Butch's form dissolved into ash, slipping through his fingers.

"Easy, Hung." Chien's voice cut through the darkness, pulling Hung back to the present. "It's just a dream."

Hung gasped for air, his chest heaving as his eyes snapped open. His heart raced, but the terror of the nightmare still clung to him. The pain in his body was real, but the nightmare... it lingered, a constant reminder of the horrors he couldn't escape.

"You've been asleep for hours," Chien said softly, resting a hand on Hung's shoulder. "Your body needs time to heal."

Hung blinked, the weight of Chien's words sinking in. His mind was foggy, his body heavy with fatigue. "It was just a dream," he whispered, his voice hoarse and broken.

Chien nodded, his expression softening. "But you're safe now. Rest, Little Fish."

The name cut through Hung, stirring something deep inside him. Little Fish—it felt like a cruel reminder of the boy he had once been, weak and scared. But that wasn't who he was anymore. He had fought. He had survived.

He wasn't just the frightened boy running from his past.

Chien seemed to sense Hung's thoughts. "You're not a little fish anymore," he said quietly, a hint of pride in his voice. "You've earned a new name. From now on, you'll be Little Dragon."

The words hung in the air, and Hung felt his heart swell with emotion. Little Dragon. The name resonated within him, a symbol of the strength he had yet to fully realize. He wasn't there yet, but he was on the path. Chien believed it, and slowly, Hung was starting to believe it too.

He nodded weakly, the name settling into his bones like a promise. Little Dragon. It was a name that carried weight, a name that held power.

Chien stood, his movements fluid as he turned toward the door. "Rest now," he said gently. "You'll need your strength for what's to come."

Hung wanted to ask what Chien meant, but the exhaustion was too much to fight. His body was heavy, and sleep pulled at him once more. The pain had receded into the background, eclipsed by the promise of the name that echoed in his mind.

Little Dragon.

As sleep claimed him, Hung felt a new resolve building within him. His body was broken, but his spirit was stronger. He would become the Little Dragon, and nothing would stand in his way.

CHAPTER 19

TRAINING WITH SHADOWS

"The mind is everything. What you think, you become." — Buddha

Hung's eyes fluttered open, the world around him slowly coming into focus. His body was a battlefield, every muscle aching, every bone reminding him of the fragility of his existence. He exhaled sharply, the pain settling deep into his bones. Each breath, each movement, was a struggle—a test of will against the gnawing agony that refused to leave his side. Yet he forced himself up, each motion deliberate, his resolve hardening with every wince of pain. Survival was the only option.

Chien stood nearby, watching with a mixture of approval and concern. His eyes followed Hung's struggle to rise, but he remained silent, his expression unreadable.

"The medicine is working," Chien said finally, his tone as steady as ever. He handed Hung another dose of the bitter concoction they'd been using to treat his wounds.

Hung accepted the cup, grimacing as the sharp taste burned its way down his throat, but he drank it without hesitation. Pain was nothing new—this was simply another battle.

"How long was I out?" Hung rasped, his throat dry and voice hoarse.

"Not long," Nhât responded from across the room, his hands busy cleaning fish with methodical precision.

The rhythmic scrape of the knife against scales filled the room, a sound that was oddly soothing, grounding them in a routine that felt comforting despite the chaos outside.

Nhât's presence brought a sense of calm to Hung.

His friend's quiet competence and focus reminded him that there was still a world outside his own pain—a world where tasks were completed, and life continued.

Nhât approached, offering Hung a wooden cup filled with water. "Drink slowly," he instructed, his voice firm yet kind. Hung obeyed, the cool liquid providing brief relief from the dryness that scratched at his throat.

Chien moved to stand behind Nhât, his eyes lingering on Hung with a mix of expectation and caution. "We don't have much medicine left," Chien said. "We'll use it sparingly, but it should last long enough." The unspoken implication hung in the air: time was a luxury they didn't have.

Hung took another sip, savoring the simple comfort of the water. It was moments like these—brief, fleeting moments of normalcy—that allowed him to push through the pain, to find some sense of control. Nhât offered a small smile, and Hung returned it weakly.

"You'll get used to it," Hung muttered, his attempt at humor masking the constant throbbing in his body.

"I couldn't believe it when Chien asked me to stay," Nhât said, his voice brightening. "But I'm glad I did."

Hung nodded. "Chien sees potential in people," he replied. It was a statement of fact. Chien had a gift for recognizing strength in others, even when they couldn't see it in themselves.

Chien's approving nod followed. "Nhât will join us on our next voyage," Chien said. "He's adaptable and trustworthy. He'll be a valuable addition." The words carried weight, and Hung felt a surge of pride. Despite the pain, despite the struggle, he was part of something larger—something important.

Chien handed him a strip of sweetened meat, and Hung devoured it, the rush of sugar providing a brief but powerful burst of energy. For a moment, the pain dulled, and he allowed himself to enjoy the simple pleasure of food.

After the meal, Chien handed Hung a crutch, sturdy and well-crafted. "Your leg is injured, but it's not severe," Chien explained. "Use this to keep your weight off it. You'll heal in time."

Hung stood slowly, testing the crutch and shifting his weight cautiously. A dull ache radiated through his leg, but he steadied himself. The pain was constant—a reminder of the battle he had fought, a reminder that he was still alive.

"There's more food outside. Eat well so your body can heal," Chien instructed. The promise of more sustenance was a lifeline, and Hung followed the command eagerly.

Every bite brought a little more strength, a little more life, back into his body.

When he finished, he joined Nhât at the basin, helping with the dishes. The simple task provided a sense of normalcy, grounding him in the routine. Each motion was repetitive, but it felt good to contribute, to be useful again.

Chien appeared beside them, moving with his usual silent grace. "Here," he said, handing Hung another dose of the bitter medicine. Hung took it without hesitation, grimacing at the taste but grateful for its effects.

"We're heading to the east side of town today," Chien announced, pulling a satchel from beneath the counter and slinging it over his shoulder. "We have work to do."

Hung adjusted to the rhythm of the crutch, determined to keep up with the group. The pain in his leg throbbed with each step, but he wouldn't let it slow him down. Not now.

They arrived at an abandoned house on the outskirts of town, the jungle creeping ever closer to the rundown structure. The stench of rotting fish and urine hit Hung immediately, the sharpness of the smell making him gag.

The house was in shambles, serving as temporary shelter for the homeless and a hideout for local thieves. Its dilapidated state mirrored the harsh reality of their world.

"Today, we play a special game," Chien announced, gathering the group around. "I call it 'Tag the Man.' It's a lesson in stealth and awareness—skills you'll need for hunting and tracking when we reach the island."

The children, including Hung and Nhât, listened intently. Chien's voice had a mesmerizing quality that drew them in, making them eager to prove themselves.

From his satchel, Chien pulled out four metal tubes, each one sharpened at the end.

"Hold them carefully," Chien instructed. "They're spring-loaded. If you strike with enough force, the tube will turn red. That's how you'll know you've succeeded."

Hung's eyes narrowed as he studied the tool in his hand. Despite his injury, the thrill of the challenge sparked a fire in him. He wanted to be part of this—to prove he was still capable.

"Little Dragon, you're injured. You can sit this one out," Chien said, addressing Hung with the new nickname that resonated deeply within him.

"I can do it," Hung insisted, his voice steady despite the pain in his leg. The name "Little Dragon" filled him with pride, a symbol of his strength.

Chien nodded, accepting his determination. "Very well. Let's see what you can do."

They moved through the marketplace, the crowd providing cover for their mission. Hung hobbled on his crutch, his eyes scanning for his target. Each step sent a jolt of pain through his leg, but his mind remained focused.

His target was a middle-aged man, moving slowly through the busy market. Hung moved carefully, blending into the crowd as best he could. His father's teachings echoed in his mind: *"Control your mind, and you control the fight."*

As he approached the man, Hung pretended to trip, falling into the man's arms. In the same motion, he jabbed the tube into the man's hand. The man flinched, barely noticing the small puncture before walking away.

A moment later, the man collapsed into the crowd, unconscious.

Hung's heart raced, a mixture of relief and pride surging through him. He had done it.

One by one, the others returned, their tubes marked with red, signaling their success. Chien inspected each one, nodding approvingly. "Good work," he praised. Even Hung, despite his injury, had managed to succeed.

"We'll head into the jungle and cross over to the southern part of town," Chien said. "I have business there, and then we'll return to the boat to prepare for our journey."

The journey was long and exhausting, each step a reminder of the day's exertions. They arrived at a rundown building on the southern edge of town. Chien knocked on the door, and they were led inside. The air was thick with the smell of alcohol and sweat.

"If anyone comes in, bang on the table. I'll hear you through the door," Chien instructed, disappearing into a back room. The gravity of his words weighed on the children, but they nodded in understanding.

While they waited, a woman behind the bar brought them small cakes. The sweetness was a welcome reprieve from the day's hardships, but there was an unease in the air that none of them could shake.

When Chien emerged, his satchel was heavier, his expression unreadable. They followed him back outside into the cool evening air, the night sky glittering with stars overhead. The walk back to the shop was quiet, the only sound the occasional call of nocturnal creatures.

Hung's leg throbbed with each step, but he kept silent. He wouldn't show weakness.

Chien noticed his struggle. "Come on, Little Dragon,"

Chien said softly, crouching down to offer Hung a ride on his back. Hung hesitated, but Chien's gentle smile reassured him. Handing his crutch to Nhât, Hung climbed onto Chien's back, feeling the warmth and strength of the older man as they moved along the path.

As they approached the shop, something slipped from Hung's pocket, glinting in the moonlight. Chien noticed but said nothing, discreetly picking it up and tucking it into his pocket for later.

Once inside, Chien gently let Hung down into his hammock, handing him a small bottle of liquid. "Drink this. It will help you sleep through the night."

Hung took the bottle and nodded gratefully. "Thank you, sir," he murmured, his voice heavy with exhaustion.

He drank the medicine in slow sips, feeling the warmth spread through his body as it began to take effect.

"You did well today, Little Dragon," Chien said, resting his hand on the back of Hung's head in a rare gesture of affection. His voice was soft, carrying a tone of pride.

"You've earned your rest."

"Yes, sir," Hung whispered, closing his eyes as the day's events replayed in his mind. The thrill of success mixed with the pain of his injury, but in that moment, the exhaustion overtook everything else. He drifted off to sleep, comforted by Chien's words and the gentle sway of the hammock beneath him.

Chien lingered for a moment, watching over Hung as he slept, before quietly stepping out of the shop. He paused at the doorway, looking up at the night sky, his gaze fixed on the stars that twinkled above. The sight of the stars stirred something deep within him, a flood of memories from long ago. His jaw tightened, and tears welled up in his eyes as the grief he had buried so deeply resurfaced.

He wiped his eyes quickly, fists clenched at his sides. There was no room for weakness—not now, not with everything that lay ahead. The night air was cool against his skin as he walked down the dirt road, his steps growing heavier with each passing moment. Anger and sorrow churned inside him, a storm brewing beneath his calm exterior.

As Chien disappeared into the shadows, the flickering light from the shop behind him slowly faded. The children slept soundly, unaware of the turmoil within the man who had become their leader, their guide, and their protector.

CHAPTER 20

BREAKING BOUNDARIES

*"Do not go where the path may lead, go
instead where there is no path and leave
a trail." — Ralph Waldo Emerson*

Chien stood at the entrance of the tavern, his calloused hand resting on the rough, weathered wood of the door. The scent of stale liquor, sweat, and something darker—something festering—filled the air like a shroud. This place had become his refuge, a dimly lit, smoke-choked sanctuary where he could drown his regrets in cheap wine and forget, if only for a while.

But tonight, the tavern felt stifling, as if the very air inside was trying to choke the life out of him, mirroring the chaos that had taken root in his soul.

He hesitated, taking a deep breath as he pressed his forehead against the door. The rough wood bit into his skin, grounding him for a fleeting moment. With a sigh that felt more like surrender, Chien pushed the door open and stepped into the dim, smoke-filled room. The noise hit him immediately—a wall of drunken voices clashing, loud, raucous laughter, and the grating scrape of chairs across the uneven wooden floor. The cacophony seemed to rise up from the floorboards, filling the space with an oppressive energy that clung to him like a second skin.

The tavern was a pit of misery, every sound an echo of the turmoil gnawing at Chien's heart. He moved toward the bar, each step heavy with the weight of guilt, shame, and the memories that plagued him. His feet dragged across the wooden floor, the familiar ache in his ribs a dull throb that matched the deeper ache in his chest. He tossed a few coins onto the counter, his hand trembling slightly as the barman slid a jug of rice wine toward him.

Without hesitation, he grabbed it, downing the bitter liquid in a single gulp. The burn in his throat was sharp, momentarily distracting him from the storm inside.

But no matter how much he drank, it couldn't silence the voices in his head.

Memories of his failures rose to the surface, crashing into him like waves on a stormy sea. His hands shook as he reached for more wine, but the storm within only grew.

The guilt weighed heavier with each passing moment, suffocating him.

"Awww… does the old man miss his mommy?"

The voice was mocking, slurred by too much alcohol but sharp enough to cut through the haze. Chien stiffened, his grip tightening around the jug. His heart pounded, the anger flaring hot inside him, but he forced himself to stay still. He had faced worse. But the alcohol had stripped away his defenses, leaving him exposed.

"Hey, sissy man, why are you ignoring me?"

The voice was closer now, laced with menace. Chien could feel the heat of the man's breath on his neck, rancid with the stench of sweat and tobacco. Then, a hand clamped down on his shoulder, the fingers digging painfully into his flesh. His heart raced, his muscles coiling tight like springs ready to snap. Slowly, he turned, his body tensed for what was to come.

The man leered at him, broad-shouldered and reeking of arrogance. He was taller, younger, and clearly eager for a fight. Chien could feel the tavern's attention shift toward them, the drunken conversations fading as the crowd sensed the tension.

But the man had no idea what he had just unleashed.

In a fluid motion, Chien swung his right arm, his fist connecting with the man's chin with a crack that echoed across the room. The brute's head snapped back, spit and blood flying as he stumbled, dazed. The tavern fell into stunned silence, eyes wide, breaths held.

Before the man could react, Chien followed up with a sharp chop to the man's forearm. The satisfying pop of dislocated bone was accompanied by a howl of pain, the man's arm falling limp. Chien didn't hesitate. He stepped forward and delivered a crushing blow to the man's solar plexus, driving the air from his lungs. The man crumpled to the floor, unconscious before he hit the ground.

Chien stood over him, panting, his vision swimming as the adrenaline faded. His body screamed, every muscle aching, but he remained on his feet, barely holding on.

The tavern was silent. Before Chien could catch his breath, three more men rushed at him. Their footsteps pounded, and in a heartbeat, they were on him. Fists and feet struck, each blow sending pain shooting through him. His head slammed into a wooden table, the impact exploding like fireworks behind his eyes. His ribs throbbed, each breath labored as his vision blurred.

He tried to fight back, but the alcohol dulled his reflexes. His movements were slow, sluggish. Another punch connected with his side, and Chien felt the air leave his lungs. His body refused to move as the world faded in and out of focus.

The last thing he saw was a boot coming toward his face.

Chien wasn't sure how long he had been unconscious when he came to. His body was on fire, every muscle screaming in pain. His head throbbed violently, and his mouth tasted of blood. He tried to move, but his limbs refused to cooperate. Small hands lifted him, dragging him. It took a moment to recognize the voices calling his name.

Hung… Nhât… They were here.

A violent cough seized him, sending blood splattering. His body hung limp as the children pulled him from the tavern. The world blurred, the sharp pain of each bump adding to the nausea twisting his stomach.

The children struggled. He could feel their small hands gripping his arms, their frail frames barely managing to support his weight as they dragged him toward the harbor.

Guilt twisted in his chest, sharper than any injury. He had failed them. Again.

By the time they reached the small shop, Chien was on the verge of passing out again. His vision swam as Nhât and Hung laid him in a hammock. The pain in his body was overwhelming, but it was nothing compared to the weight of his shame. He could barely lift his head as Nhât pressed medicine to his lips, tipping it between the fits of coughing. The liquid did little to numb the fire raging inside him.

Darkness closed in, and Chien let it take him.

When he awoke, it was to sharp, searing pain. His head throbbed, and every muscle felt torn apart. He cursed, trying to shift, but the effort sent fresh waves of agony through him. His ribs screamed in protest, the bruises throbbing like fresh wounds.

"Stupid," he muttered, lying still.

The fight, the alcohol—none of it had helped. He had been reckless, foolish. How could he protect Hung and Nhât if he couldn't protect himself?

A memory surfaced—her face, calm and steady. She had been his anchor. Now, she was his greatest regret.

The scars on his body bore her name, each one a reminder of how he had failed. And now, he had failed the children. The guilt was a weight, pressing down, making it hard to breathe.

"Coward." The word echoed, louder than the pain. Powerless to save her. Powerless to stop the fight.

Powerless to protect the children. What good was he?

He thrashed weakly, trying to escape the memory, but it clung to him.

Chien woke with a start. Hung was beside him, wiping sweat from his brow. The boy's face was tight with worry.

Nhât must have helped lift him into the hammock. Chien couldn't meet their eyes. He had let them down.

He forced himself to sit up, trembling with the effort.

Slowly, he ate the food beside him, each swallow tasting of ash. He had to regain his strength—for them.

But when he tried to stand, his legs gave way, sending him crashing to the floor. Pain shot through his ribs, and his vision darkened. The last thing he heard was Nhât's voice, calling his name in a panic.

Then, there was nothing.

CHAPTER 21

FIRE IN THE NIGHT

"Out of the frying pan, into the fire." — J.R.R. Tolkien

The midday sun streamed through the small window, casting a beam of light that slanted across Chien's battered body as he lay in the hammock. Each breath was a sharp reminder of the toll he had taken, pain flaring in his ribs like jagged shards. The scent of medicinal herbs clung to the air, offering a faint comfort amidst his discomfort. His head pounded in sync with his heartbeat, and for a brief moment, he was disoriented.

But the murmur of voices outside and the familiar smell brought him back to reality.

The children had saved him—again.

His fists clenched involuntarily, nails digging into his palms as the weight of failure settled over him. How many times had they needed to save him when it should have been the other way around? **Reckless. Weak.** A leader shouldn't collapse when his people need him most, yet here he was, broken and bruised, while they had carried on without him.

Shame curled in his chest. What kind of leader allows children—survivors who had looked to him for guidance—

to fend for themselves? He had crumbled when they needed him, unable to even stand.

Closing his eyes, Chien tried to push away the memories, but they clung to him like shadows. Her face, so vivid, surfaced in his mind—a face he had tried to forget but never could. She had been his anchor, the one who kept him grounded. Now, she was a constant reminder of his greatest regret.

A bitter taste filled his mouth. **Coward.** The word echoed in his mind, much like it had on the night she'd walked away. He had begged her, pleaded with her to run away with him, to escape together. But she had made her choice, and he hadn't been strong enough to stop her. **Not strong enough to save her.**

Now, he had failed again.

Pushing through the pain, Chien forced himself to sit up. His body screamed in protest, every muscle tight with agony, but he couldn't lie there any longer. The children were depending on him. They had trusted him to lead them, and he couldn't let them down again. Not after everything they'd been through.

The room swayed as he sat up, dizziness flooding his senses, but he gripped the edge of the hammock and steadied himself. His vision swam, and his head throbbed, but he fought through it. Weakness wasn't an option. Not now.

He glanced around the small room. The children had done well, better than he could have expected. They had kept everything in order, followed his teachings, and cared for him when he couldn't even care for himself. A surge of pride filled him, but it was quickly followed by a sharper, more painful emotion—guilt. **They shouldn't have had to learn this way.**

His thoughts drifted to the jungle ahead—a dark, foreboding place that loomed in his mind. It was where they were headed next, and nothing he had taught them could fully prepare them for what waited there.

The predators in the jungle weren't just animals. They were men—dangerous men who wouldn't hesitate to kill them all.

A chill ran through him at the thought. Could he protect them? Was he strong enough? Or would he fail them again, like he had failed her?

No. Not this time.

Chien's fists tightened, his resolve hardening. He would lead them through whatever trials awaited, no matter the cost. He had already lost too much, but he couldn't afford to lose them too.

The door creaked, and Hung entered, his face a mixture of concern and determination. He carried a tray of food—fish, crab meat, and water—and beside it, a small bottle of medicine. Hung placed the tray on the table next to the hammock and, with careful precision, wiped the sweat from Chien's brow with a damp cloth.

"You need to rest," Hung said softly, his voice barely above a whisper.

Chien shook his head, the motion sending a fresh wave of dizziness through him. "There's no time for rest," he replied, his voice firmer than his body felt. "We need to keep moving."

Hung frowned, uncertainty flickering in his eyes. "But—"

"I'll be fine," Chien interrupted, his voice rough but insistent. His body rebelled against the lie, but he couldn't show weakness. Not now. "You've done well, Little Dragon, but there's still work to be done. We're not safe yet."

Hung hesitated for a moment, then gave a small nod.

Though he didn't argue, Chien could see the doubt in the boy's eyes. Hung was strong, stronger than any child should have to be, but the weight of responsibility was pressing down on him. Chien couldn't let the burden fall entirely on the children. They had done enough. It was time for him to step up.

As Hung left the room to join the others outside, Chien let out a shuddering breath. His gaze fell on the tray of food, but the guilt in his chest made it hard to even consider eating. The children had followed his instructions, saved him from his own weakness. But it wasn't their job to save him. It was his job to save them.

He had to be better. He had to be stronger.

Gripping the side of the hammock, Chien forced himself to his feet. The room tilted dangerously as his ribs protested every movement, but he gritted his teeth and pushed through the pain. He couldn't let them see him like this—broken and weak. He had to be the leader they needed, the protector they believed in.

The midday sun hit him hard as he stepped outside, the brightness forcing him to squint against the harsh light.

The salty air of the harbor filled his lungs as he steadied himself, the sounds of the children hard at work reaching his ears. Kim and Sen were loading supplies onto the High Tides, their small bodies moving quickly between the dock and the ship. Nhât was gutting fish nearby, his hands working with practiced precision.

Chien paused in the doorway, watching them for a moment. They had become more than just survivors. They were a family. His family. And he wouldn't let the jungle take them. Not after everything they had survived.

But the jungle… it was a shadow looming over their future. A place of unimaginable dangers. They had no choice, though. They needed the medicine the jungle offered, or they wouldn't survive much longer.

He would lead them through it. No matter what.

Chien approached Nhât, placing a hand on the boy's shoulder. "Where's Hung?"

Nhât startled slightly, nearly dropping the fish he was cleaning. "He went back to the market after checking on you," Nhât muttered, irritation creeping into his voice as he bent to pick up the fish scraps.

Chien nodded, hiding a smile. "Very well. Carry on."

He walked toward the road, each step sending spikes of pain through his body. But he pushed forward, determined not to falter. Halfway to the marketplace, he spotted Hung limping toward him. The boy's face was drawn tight with tension, his eyes fixed on the ground.

When he looked up and saw Chien, his pace quickened despite his limp.

"You didn't have to come," Hung said, though the relief in his eyes was unmistakable.

Chien offered a faint smile. "I'm sure you were fine. What happened at the market?"

Hung's gaze dropped to the ground. "The bodies..." His voice wavered. "They're washing up along the shore. More than the harbor authority can clear."

Chien's stomach tightened. The boy's words painted a grim picture—bodies, bloated and lifeless, drifting to shore like remnants of a forgotten tragedy. He could see the strain it had placed on Hung, the way his hands shook, the weight of death heavy on him.

"It's grim," Chien said softly, placing a hand on Hung's shoulder. "But we need to stay focused. Let's head back to the boat before it gets worse."

As they walked in silence, Chien's mind raced. The jungle was waiting, filled with dangers they couldn't yet fathom. But now, the sight of bodies washing ashore weighed on him. It wasn't just another obstacle—it was a warning.

When they reached the harbor, the sight stole Chien's breath. Bodies—bloated, twisted, pale—floated at the waterline, their limbs tangled in the debris. The stench of decay hung heavy in the air, mixing with the salty breeze.

Seabirds circled above, their cries sharp and mournful as they picked at the remains.

Chien's pulse quickened, dread pooling in his stomach. **This wasn't just a threat. It was a sign of what was coming.**

"We don't have much time," Chien muttered, his voice tight with urgency. "We need to leave. Now."

The children were already moving quickly, their faces grim as they loaded the last supplies onto the boat. There were no questions, no hesitation—only the understanding that they were running out of time.

"We leave with the tide," Chien ordered, his voice louder now, cutting through the eerie silence. "We're not staying to find out what's coming."

Nhât and the others moved faster, securing ropes, checking the supplies. Their urgency mirrored the growing unease in Chien's chest.

As he stepped onto the boat, his gaze lingered on the shore, where the bodies bobbed in the water like grim markers of what awaited them. Something was coming.

And they needed to be gone before it arrived.

CHAPTER 22

SILENT STRUGGLES

*"The quieter you become, the more
you can hear."* — Ram Dass

Chien could feel the air thickening, as if the very atmosphere itself was pressing down on them. The tide wasn't just coming—it was surging, dragging with it bloated, grotesque bodies that bobbed on the water's surface like dark omens. He stared out at the waves, watching as the sea delivered a macabre reminder of how many had already been claimed by its unforgiving depths. The sight was horrifying, yet it wasn't fear that gripped him. It was urgency. A gnawing awareness that time was slipping away.

"Move!" Chien's voice cut through the stillness like a blade, slicing into the oppressive silence that had settled over their group. There was no room for hesitation.

The harbor wasn't just a place to leave behind—it was on the verge of becoming a graveyard. Every second they lingered brought them closer to joining the bodies in the tide.

He glanced down at Hung, who hobbled beside him, the boy's leg clearly paining him. Hung's limp slowed them, but not once did the boy complain. His face was set in grim determination, each step a testament to his refusal to give in to weakness. Chien's chest tightened with pride, but there was no time to reflect. Not now. Not with death so close behind.

As they pushed forward, Chien's mind raced ahead, calculating their next move. They had drilled for emergencies like this. **Tactical Training (TT)** wasn't just about combat—it was about preparation, efficiency, and speed. The children knew their roles, but the stakes had never been this high. The tide was no longer just water; it was a harbinger of death, bringing with it a stench of rot and decay that hung heavy in the air.

The harbor loomed ahead, and Chien's breath quickened as they neared it. The children had already begun loading the boat, their small faces hardened with the knowledge that failure wasn't an option. Supplies were packed with military precision, the kind that only came from relentless training and repetition. Chien paused for a brief moment, his heart swelling with pride. They were young, but they were capable. They had learned well.

"You've done well," Chien said, his voice momentarily soft before the urgency crept back in. "But we're not safe yet. The tide's coming fast, and we need to leave before the harbor is overrun."

The children didn't speak. They nodded and returned to their tasks, their movements sharp and purposeful.

They understood the gravity of the situation—there was no room for mistakes. **Tactical Training (TT)** had prepared them for this moment, where survival depended on how quickly they could act.

As Chien bent down to grab the last of the medicine, his fingers brushed against something cold and metallic. He pulled it from his pocket—a small silver cylinder, smooth and heavier than it looked. His brow furrowed.

It was one of the items that had fallen from Hung's pack earlier, but now, in the fading light of the harbor, something about it felt different.

"Hung!" Chien called, his voice cutting through the clamor of their preparations.

Hung appeared almost immediately, his breathing heavy but his expression focused. Despite the boy's limp, he was alert, ready for whatever task was next.

"Yes, sir?" Hung's voice was steady, but Chien could see the strain in his eyes.

Chien held up the cylinder. "Where did you get this? And do you have more of them?"

Hung's gaze flickered with confusion as he glanced at the object. "I have a few more in my pack, sir. I didn't think they were important."

Chien's eyes narrowed. "Bring them. Every single one."

Without hesitation, Hung turned and sprinted back toward the boat, his injured leg making the run awkward, but the boy didn't slow. Chien watched him go, his mind working furiously to piece together the puzzle of the cylinder. **Knowledge Transfer (KT)** wasn't just about physical lessons—it was about recognizing value in the unexpected. Even the smallest object could shift the balance of survival.

The tide was close now, the bodies drifting in with unsettling speed. Dark shapes floated just beneath the surface, their grotesque forms twisting and turning with each wave. Chien turned away from the sight, his stomach churning as the smell hit him—decay and death, thick in the air.

"Load the rest!" Chien barked, his voice rising in urgency. The children moved faster, their faces tightening as they heard the edge in his tone. They knew what was coming. The tide would reach the harbor soon, and when it did, no one would leave.

Hung returned moments later, a bundle of silver cylinders clutched in his arms. His face was drawn, his earlier confusion replaced with grim understanding. He handed the objects to Chien without a word.

"We'll figure this out later," Chien said, stuffing the cylinders into his pack. "Right now, we need to get out of here."

The wind, weak and inconsistent, barely stirred the sails. Chien cursed under his breath as he grabbed one of the oars, setting the example. The children followed, each taking an oar and paddling in unison. Their muscles strained with the effort, but the boat was slow. The tide was faster.

Then, the bodies reached them.

The first impact was sickening—a dull thud as a bloated corpse collided with the hull. The sound echoed in the stillness, a grotesque drumbeat that sent shivers down Chien's spine. More followed, each body bumping against the wood, their lifeless forms twisting and turning in the dark water.

Chien's grip on the oar tightened, his knuckles white as he pushed harder. "Come on!" he shouted, his voice hoarse. "Keep paddling!"

The children responded, their strokes becoming frantic as they fought to break free of the tide. But the bodies kept coming, pressing against the boat like a grim reminder of what awaited them if they failed.

Just as the weight of despair began to settle over Chien, the current caught them. The boat surged forward, pulled by a sudden rush of water that carried them away from the harbor and its horrors. Relief flooded through him, but it was short-lived. They had escaped the tide, but the sea held its own dangers.

As the boat drifted into calmer waters, Chien's muscles screamed in protest. He dropped the oar, letting out a long breath. They had made it. Barely.

Hung stood beside him, silent, his face pale but determined. Chien looked at him and saw the boy's exhaustion. But more than that, he saw resilience—a strength that had been forged in the fires of hardship.

Hung wasn't just surviving. He was learning. Growing.

"You did well," Chien said quietly, his voice carrying over the soft lapping of the waves. "I know it wasn't easy, but you kept your head. That's what matters."

Hung didn't respond at first. His gaze was fixed on the dark horizon, but there was a flicker of emotion in his eyes—gratitude, perhaps, or something deeper.

"Thank you, sir," he said softly, his voice steady despite everything they had just endured.

Chien gave him a nod. "Go rest. You've earned it."

Hung hesitated, glancing at Chien with concern. "What about you, sir?"

"I'll be fine," Chien replied, his voice rough with exhaustion. "Go."

Reluctantly, Hung turned and made his way below deck. Chien watched him go, the boy's figure disappearing into the shadows. As soon as Hung was gone, Chien sagged against the railing, his body finally giving in to the weariness that had been building.

He pulled the silver cylinder from his pocket, holding it up to the faint light of the moon. The cool metal felt heavy in his hand, its weight a reminder of the mystery that still lingered. There was something important here— something that could change everything. But for now, that mystery would have to wait.

Chien's eyes scanned the horizon. The wind had picked up, pushing them farther out to sea, away from the nightmare they had just escaped. The harbor was nothing more than a distant glow now, shrinking with each passing moment. They had survived the first trial, but Chien knew the real dangers still lay ahead.

He tightened his grip on the cylinder, his jaw clenching as he stared out into the darkness. Whatever this object was, it held a secret—a secret they would need to uncover before they faced the jungle. Before they faced what was coming.

For now, though, they sailed on. Into the unknown. Into whatever awaited them in the deep, uncharted waters ahead.

CHAPTER 23

CONFESSIONS OF THE SEA

"The truth is rarely pure and never simple." — Oscar Wilde

Hung awoke to a sharp knock reverberating through the cabin door. His eyes blinked open, and his senses immediately became alert. The urgency behind the knock jolted the other two boys awake, and they scrambled out of their bunks. Hung shifted, testing his leg. A slight ache lingered, but it was a muted pain, more tolerable than the day before. He pressed his foot flat against the floor, cautious but eager. A wave of satisfaction rushed through him—he could stand without the crutch.

For the first time in days, he felt a spark of freedom. He was shedding his weakness, leaving the crutch behind like a skin he no longer needed. Despite the limp that persisted, Hung stood taller, his body more in tune with the rhythm of the ship beneath him.

As they emerged onto the deck, the sunlight greeted them, casting a golden hue across the calm waters. The wind carried the salty tang of the sea, and for a moment, Hung breathed it in deeply, savoring the tranquility. But that peace was short-lived. He caught sight of Chien, standing with his back straight, his gaze sharp as it tracked their movements. When Chien's eyes met Hung's, he nodded—brief, but approving. It wasn't just a nod at his physical recovery, but a recognition of something deeper, something growing within Hung.

Hung returned the gesture, pride swelling in his chest. Yet beneath that pride, a flicker of doubt gnawed at him. His body was healing, but his mind—his spirit— still felt incomplete. He had tasted small victories in his recovery, but there was a long road ahead. Each step toward physical strength only served as a reminder that the true battle, the one within, had just begun.

On deck, a simple breakfast was laid out—rice and salted fish. Chien's methodical nature extended even to meals, and Hung noted how the small, sturdy table was bolted to the deck, keeping it steady amid the rolling sea.

As they ate in silence, the ship creaked rhythmically with each wave, a serene soundtrack to their meal. The food was humble, but it filled their bellies, providing strength for the tasks ahead. As Hung chewed, his thoughts wandered to the unknowns that awaited them.

The calm sea before him belied the storms that surely lay ahead. His fingers tightened around his bowl, a subtle reflection of the tension building in his chest. There was more to come—he could feel it.

Chien, looking worn from the night's watch, handed the helm to Kim with a few quiet instructions. Kim's sharp nod and quick takeover of duties spoke volumes of his experience as a young sailor. His calm efficiency reminded Hung of the discipline needed not just on a ship, but in life. Kim's authority was understated yet unmistakable. He commanded with a quiet precision, and the boys listened carefully as he assigned their tasks for the day. There were no complaints, no wasted movements.

Each boy took to his duty with the single-minded focus of someone determined to prove their worth.

Hung worked with a methodical intensity, scrubbing the deck and tightening the ropes that held the barrels. His hands moved automatically, but his mind buzzed with restless thoughts. Could the barrels be secured more efficiently? Was there a better way to keep the ship running smoothly? The questions nagged at him, hinting at a deeper understanding he hadn't yet grasped.

There was something there—some knowledge waiting to reveal itself, if only he could see the pattern.

As the sun climbed higher, the ship settled into a steady rhythm. Kim, ever vigilant, found new tasks to keep the ship in pristine order. Hung welcomed the work, the physicality grounding him even as his thoughts churned with anticipation. Around midday, Sen appeared by his side, leading him to a quieter spot on the deck.

With quiet determination, Sen spread out several sheets of paper and placed a pencil in Hung's hand.

"Let's continue," she said softly, her tone encouraging but firm. Hung frowned at the letters scrawled across the page, their shapes twisting in his mind like foreign symbols refusing to settle. Each line, each curve felt like a battle. But Sen was patient, guiding him through the basics again, her fingers lightly correcting his grip on the pencil. The sun warmed their backs as they worked, the sound of the waves providing a steady backdrop to his learning.

"You're improving," Sen said, a small smile tugging at her lips as Hung managed to scratch out his name correctly.

Hung stared at the letters, his name barely legible. "It's harder than I thought," he admitted, his frustration palpable.

"Yes," she replied gently, "but you'll get there. Just keep practicing."

Hung nodded, determination hardening his resolve. He knew mastering reading and writing was essential. If he wanted to be more than just a fighter, if he wanted to be truly strong, he needed to conquer these challenges. Yet with every small victory came the daunting realization of how much he still didn't know. This was just the beginning, and the weight of that realization settled heavily on his shoulders. There was a vast world of knowledge beyond him—one that the three masters he had yet to meet would unlock. Hung felt that this journey was more than physical survival—it was a quest to understand himself, the world, and the forces that shaped both.

After the lesson, they returned to their routine. Hung worked with more focus now, each task performed with a sense of purpose. But just as the mundane rhythm of the day settled in, Chien approached him at the bow.

The air seemed to shift as Chien's presence commanded Hung's attention.

"Little Dragon," Chien's voice was steady, but Hung heard the weight behind it. There was something different in his tone—a gravity that made Hung pause.

Hung wiped the sweat from his brow and leaned against a nearby crate, sensing that this conversation would be more than routine. "Yes, sir."

For a moment, Chien didn't speak. His eyes drifted to the horizon, scanning the distance as if searching for the right words. Hung waited, his muscles tensing in anticipation.

Chien broke the silence with a confession that caught Hung off guard. "The night you found me near the marketplace—drunk, beaten—I owe you an explanation."

Hung didn't move. His respect for Chien was immense, and he didn't want to disrupt whatever was about to be shared. He remained silent, knowing instinctively that this was a moment for listening, not speaking.

Chien's voice dropped, quieter now, almost a whisper.

"There are things about my past… things I haven't told anyone. But it's time." He hesitated, then began to recount his role in a life far removed from the one he now led. A life of smuggling—people, weapons, information— along the coast. High Tides had been his vessel for these covert missions. Hung listened, his eyes widening as Chien's words painted a vivid picture of danger and secrecy. The ship he stood on wasn't just a lifeline for them now—it had always been Chien's connection to a world of shadows and peril.

Chien paused, his voice catching slightly as he described a mission that changed everything. A young woman, Tien, disguised as a prostitute, had been smuggled into an American military base. She was more than just a partner in the field—she had been Chien's partner in life, the mother of Kim and Sen.

Hung's chest tightened as he processed this revelation. Chien's voice grew softer, more distant, as if the memories themselves were a weight he had carried for too long.

Tien had been captured, tortured, and finally killed, her body discarded like refuse. Chien had found her too late, her last words a whisper of where to find Sen.

Hung stood frozen, feeling the weight of Chien's grief pressing down on him. He wanted to say something, anything, but words felt inadequate in the face of such loss. Instead, he did the only thing that felt right. He walked over to Chien and wrapped his arms around him.

Chien tensed at first, but after a moment, he let himself relax into the embrace.

For a long while, they stood in silence, the only sound the gentle lapping of the waves against the hull. Hung could feel the depth of Chien's pain, a grief that had been buried beneath the surface for so long. In that quiet moment, their bond strengthened—not as master and student, but as two souls connected by shared suffering.

When Chien finally pulled away, there was a faint smile on his lips, though his eyes were still clouded with emotion. "Thank you, Little Dragon," he whispered. "I've carried this for too long."

Hung nodded, his throat too tight to speak. He watched as Chien retreated into his thoughts, the weight of the confession lifting slightly from his shoulders. The ship rocked gently beneath them, the vast expanse of the sea surrounding them like a protective embrace.

As the evening approached, the stars began to dot the sky, small pinpricks of light in the growing darkness. Chien's voice broke the silence once more, softer now.

"We're nearing land. We'll drop anchor soon. It's too dangerous to continue in the dark."

Hung nodded, understanding the caution behind Chien's words. The journey wasn't just about reaching a destination. It was about preparing for what lay ahead— mentally, physically, and spiritually. He glanced at Chien one more time, feeling a new sense of respect for the man. He had survived not just the physical challenges of life, but the emotional scars that came with them. Hung hoped that one day, he too would be strong enough to carry the weight of his past without it breaking him.

As the anchor splashed into the water, Hung took a deep breath, the cool night air filling his lungs. He looked up at the stars, each one a reminder that even in the darkest of nights, there was always a light to guide the way.

CHAPTER 24

ISLAND OF SHADOWS

"It is not the mountain we conquer, but ourselves." — Sir Edmund Hillary

The sun was still low on the horizon, but the heat was already seeping into the cabin, clinging to the air like a weight. Hung stirred, feeling the familiar stickiness of sweat on his skin. The salty scent of the sea mixed with the musty wood of the cabin, grounding him in his surroundings. As his mind slowly woke up, his stomach let out a low growl, reminding him how long it had been since his last real meal.

He sat up slowly, swinging his legs over the edge of the bunk and testing his weight on the floor. The sharp pain that had plagued his leg for days had finally faded to a dull ache. A brief wave of gratitude washed over him—his body, hardened by years of punishment and survival, had once again adapted and healed, pushing him forward.

Across the small room, Nhât and Kim were already up, preparing for the day with quiet efficiency. Their movements were methodical, almost mechanical, as if the weight of their hunger and exhaustion had long ago dulled their emotions. Hung watched them for a moment, feeling the solidarity between them. They had been through so much together, and yet here they were, still standing, still moving forward, because there was no other option.

They stepped out of the cabin, the wooden boards beneath their feet creaking as they descended toward the deck. The salty breeze hit them with a refreshing gust, momentarily clearing the haze of fatigue. Sen appeared shortly after, her eyes sharp as they scanned the horizon. But there was no sign of Chien.

"Is he still in his cabin?" Sen asked, her voice low, but edged with concern.

"I don't think so," Kim replied, glancing around.

"No, there," Nhât said, pointing toward the starboard side.

Hung followed Nhât's gaze and saw Chien. He was alone, paddling steadily toward them in the canoe they had noticed when they first set sail. The canoe glided across the water in near silence, its movement smooth and deliberate. Chien's presence in the canoe was both reassuring and unsettling, like he was leading them into something none of them could foresee.

Without a word, Chien gestured for them to join him. The boys hurried down to the beach, a mix of excitement and unease tightening in their chests. They clambered into the canoe, and as they began to drift toward the island, the full view of it opened before them—lush green trees swayed gently in the breeze, the sunlight casting dappled patterns on the water. For a moment, it looked like a paradise, untouched by the suffering they had endured.

But that illusion didn't last long.

As they approached the island, the water near the shore grew still. The sea life that had once teemed beneath the surface was now sparse, and the few fish that remained darted nervously between chunks of debris—rotting timber, rusted metal, and remnants of wrecked boats. Hung's eyes caught on something pale and brittle-looking among the wreckage. His heart lurched when he realized they were bones, scattered like discarded trash. He tore his gaze away, his stomach twisting.

The beach was worse. Deep trenches and mounds of upturned earth scarred the sand, as though the land had been torn apart and hastily stitched back together. Felled trees lay in heaps, decaying sandbags piled high beside them. The air felt heavier here, thick with an unspoken warning. Hung's instincts screamed that they shouldn't be here. But they had no choice now.

The canoe scraped against the shore, jolting Hung from his thoughts. Chien was already on his feet, his movements swift and purposeful. He slung a pack over his shoulder, tossed another to Nhât, and tied the canoe to a nearby tree with a long rope.

"Leave the canoe in the water," Chien instructed, his voice calm but firm. "It's safer that way. Animals won't get in, and it won't get damaged by the debris on the beach."

Hung observed Chien's efficiency, noting how every action served a purpose. He didn't waste words. He taught them by doing, and they followed his lead without question. The boys crouched low, gathering around him as he prepared to speak.

"Stay low whenever possible," Chien began, scanning their surroundings with practiced eyes. "We don't know if anyone's here. Assume they are. Always make sure you see them before they see you. Stay together. Got it?"

Hung nodded along with the others. Chien's words were more than a warning—they were a survival lesson, and each one settled heavily on Hung's shoulders.

"Do you see those red flags?" Chien pointed to the small markers he had placed in a rough perimeter around their landing site. "That's our boundary. Don't go past it unless I'm with you. This area is as safe as I could make it, but it's not completely secure. No one goes anywhere alone. Understand?"

"Yes, sir," the children murmured in unison.

Chien continued, his voice even but urgent. "There are many creatures here—most of them dangerous. Some are venomous, others predatory. You need to be aware of your surroundings at all times. Knowing where you are could be the difference between life and death."

Hung glanced toward the dense jungle, his eyes tracing the dark gaps between the trees. It felt like the shadows were watching them, shifting and moving of their own accord.

Chien led them forward, crouching as he moved toward a trench further down the beach. "We'll set up camp here," he said, his eyes constantly scanning the ground for signs of danger. The boys followed closely, imitating his movements. The trench stretched along the beach like a scar, a reminder of the violence that had once consumed this land.

"Be cautious in these trenches," Chien warned. "They were dug by soldiers, and some are still rigged with traps.

I've marked the ones I found, but there could be more. I'll teach you how to use them for defense and for hunting."

Hung hesitated for a moment, staring down into the trench. The damp earth beneath his feet felt unnaturally cool as he descended the ladder. Fear gnawed at him, but he forced it down. They needed to make camp, and fear wasn't going to help. Together, they worked in silence, setting up a fire pit in the center of the trench and positioning torches around the perimeter.

Chien rummaged through his pack and pulled out a rifle, assembling it quickly. His hands moved with a quiet precision, the metal parts clicking into place.

"This is an infantry rifle," Chien explained, holding it up for them to see. "It's powerful, but it only fires one shot at a time. You'll need to reload after every shot, and it kicks hard. But it'll stop anything coming for you if you aim right."

Hung watched closely as Chien demonstrated, his mind racing with everything they had learned. The fear that had gnawed at him earlier had shifted into something more focused, more determined.

Once the camp was set, Chien planted bamboo poles along the beach, each one topped with a crude head made from driftwood.

"We'll use these for target practice tomorrow," he said. "But tonight, our only goal is to stay alive."

As the sun dipped below the horizon, the night descended quickly, bringing with it a wave of unfamiliar sounds. The jungle came alive, the rustling of leaves and the distant calls of animals echoing through the darkness.

The fire they had built flickered weakly, casting long, dancing shadows on the walls of the trench.

Hung lay on his side, his body pressed against the cool earth. Every noise outside the trench felt like a threat. His heartbeat quickened with each crackle of the fire, every snap of a twig. Time dragged on, each minute stretching into what felt like hours.

Then, without warning, a sharp metallic clank echoed through the night.

Hung froze, his breath catching in his throat. He strained his ears, listening for the source of the sound.

Chien was already on his feet, rifle in hand. He signaled for the children to stay low, his eyes scanning the darkness beyond the trench. The firelight flickered wildly, casting eerie shadows across the jungle floor.

The sound came again—closer this time.

Hung's muscles tensed, his body coiled in anticipation. The metallic clank was unmistakable, deliberate, like something was moving through the debris, inching toward them.

Chien motioned for them to move deeper into the trench, away from the firelight. They obeyed without hesitation, their movements slow and silent. The sound grew louder, more distinct, but just as suddenly as it had begun, it stopped.

The silence that followed was deafening. Hung's heart raced, his breath shallow and uneven. Chien remained at the edge of the trench, rifle raised, his eyes never leaving the darkness.

Minutes passed, each one longer than the last, until finally, Chien whispered, "It's moved on. But we'll keep watch in shifts."

The tension in Hung's chest eased slightly, but the fear remained. They arranged themselves in a rough circle, each taking turns to watch while the others rested.

Sleep came in fits and starts, each of them too aware of the danger lurking just beyond their small circle of light.

At dawn, the first rays of sunlight broke over the horizon, lifting some of the oppressive weight that had settled over them during the night. But Chien's expression was grim as he returned from checking the perimeter.

"We're not alone here," he said, his voice low but firm. "Something—or someone—was watching us last night."

The children's exhaustion was momentarily forgotten as the seriousness of the situation sunk in. They packed up their camp quickly, moving with the same quiet efficiency they had shown before.

As they climbed out of the trench, Hung couldn't shake the feeling that they were being watched. The island, once seemingly tranquil, had become a hostile, living entity. Every shadow felt like it held unseen eyes, and the weight of that presence hung over them like a cloud.

They moved cautiously along the beach, keeping to the edge of the jungle for cover. When they stumbled upon the makeshift shelter—a crude structure made of driftwood and vines—Hung's stomach twisted.

Chien approached it carefully, rifle at the ready. He paused at the entrance, listening for any sound from within. After a moment, he pulled the tattered cloth aside and stepped in.

"It's empty," Chien said when he returned, but there was a tightness in his voice that made Hung uneasy. "But someone was here, and not too long ago."

They didn't linger. Chien led them away from the shelter and deeper into the jungle, moving quickly but cautiously. The discovery of the shelter had changed everything. What was once a survival mission had become something more—now it was a race against whoever or whatever else was on this island with them.

As they pushed forward, Hung kept glancing over his shoulder. The island's unseen eyes were still on them. Watching. Waiting.

CHAPTER 25

THE TIGER'S LAIR

"Courage is not the absence of fear, but the triumph over it. The brave man is not he who does not feel afraid, but he who conquers that fear."— Nelson Mandela

Hung stirred beneath the giant banana leaf that served as his blanket, the oppressive humidity of the jungle pressing down on him like a weight. The air was thick and stifling, each breath a struggle. The jungle's sounds, once terrifying, had become part of the background, but tonight the familiar rhythm felt off.

The island, once a challenge to be conquered, now felt like a prison.

His muscles ached from the drills they'd endured earlier, but it wasn't the physical pain that kept him awake. It was the gnawing feeling in his chest. His thoughts churned, restless, and an unshakable sense of dread filled him. The end of their time here was approaching, but tonight, something felt different.

A sharp whisper pierced the darkness. "Hung!" Nhât's voice sliced through the stillness, challenging and mischievous.

Hung groaned, rolling over. "What do you want?" he growled, irritation bubbling up.

"I bet you half my breakfast you won't go get the flag I left on the beach," Nhât taunted, his voice tinged with mockery.

Hung frowned into the dark. "What flag?"

"I left it by the trench," Nhât continued, his voice teasing. "Bet you're too scared to get it."

Hung clenched his fists, his pride stung. Nhât's words cut deep, and though Chien's orders had been clear—no one was to leave the trench alone at night—Nhât's challenge pushed something primal in him.

Without another word, Hung threw the banana leaf aside and stood.

Nhât's soft laughter trailed behind him as Hung stomped away from the camp, his feet heavy with irritation and determination. The ground was uneven, making each step difficult, but Hung's pride burned brighter than his fear. He needed to prove himself.

The jungle's usual cacophony was absent. The night was still, unnervingly so. Hung's heartbeat quickened, the silence amplifying the sounds of his breath and footsteps.

He pushed forward, though every instinct screamed for him to turn back. His mind raced. Chien's words echoed in his head: *Fear is the enemy of the mind, but it can be your greatest ally if you master it.*

His clothes clung to his damp skin, the thick air making every movement sluggish. Hung forced himself to focus, to move silently through the undergrowth. Every step was a calculated risk. He knew the dangers—the jungle was alive with traps, both natural and man-made.

A sudden screech shattered the silence. Hung jumped, his heart leaping into his throat. His foot slipped on loose earth, and for a moment, he was sure he'd fall, but he caught himself just in time. His breathing quickened, his mind racing.

Stay calm. Think. Survive.

In the faint moonlight, he spotted it—the flag, fluttering softly near the trench. Relief washed over him as he grabbed it, gripping it tightly. A small smile tugged at his lips. This would show Nhât.

But the jungle wasn't done with him. A low growl rumbled through the darkness, vibrating in his bones.

Hung froze, every muscle locking as the sound grew louder, more menacing. The ground beneath him seemed to tremble as the growl was followed by deep, deliberate breaths—powerful, heavy.

His legs trembled as fear took hold. His mind scrambled for Chien's teachings. *Stay calm. Think. Survive.*

Hung turned slowly, his eyes scanning the shadows, but he saw nothing. The growl came again, this time closer, louder. And then, in the dim light, he saw it—a flash of orange fur, the unmistakable silhouette of a tiger.

Panic surged through him, his body reacting before his mind could. He bolted, his heart pounding in his chest, each step a desperate effort to escape. The jungle seemed to close in on him, the trees twisting and reaching out as if to trap him. His breath came in short, sharp gasps, and his legs burned with effort.

"HELP! HELP!" Hung's voice cracked, his screams desperate, but the jungle swallowed his cries. Behind him, the tiger's heavy footsteps grew louder, its growl more ferocious. The creature was gaining on him.

The tiger lunged. Hung felt the impact before he saw it. The force of the tiger's swipe sent him flying, crashing into the trench wall. Pain exploded in his leg, sharp and unrelenting. He screamed, his mouth filling with dirt and sand.

Stay calm. Think. Survive.

The mantra echoed in his mind, a lifeline amidst the chaos. Gritting his teeth, Hung forced himself to move. His ankle screamed in protest, but he pushed through the pain. He had to reach the spike pit. It was his only chance.

Behind him, the tiger growled again, its massive body closing in. Hung's hands trembled as he pulled himself forward, inch by inch, his vision blurring from the pain. The pit was close now. He just had to time it right.
Another growl, closer. The tiger was ready to strike.

Now.

With a final surge of strength, Hung threw himself into the trench. The tiger lunged, but its momentum carried it forward, straight into the spike pit. Hung heard the sickening crunch of bone and flesh as the beast fell, its body thrashing violently. Blood splattered across the sand as the tiger struggled, its roars growing weaker until, finally, it lay still.

A gunshot echoed through the night, snapping Hung out of his daze. Chien and the others had arrived. Chien's face was grim as he approached the pit, raising his rifle and firing one more shot to ensure the tiger was dead.

Hung sat up slowly, his body shaking. The weight of the night's events pressed down on him like a physical force. He had survived, but just barely.

Chien's voice broke the silence, harsh and unforgiving.

"Ignorance. Carelessness. Stupidity. This is how people die." His words hung in the air, and the children, including Nhât, bowed their heads in shame.

Hung stared down at his ankle, blood seeping from the gash. The pain was sharp, but what hurt more was the realization that his recklessness had nearly cost him his life. He had allowed his pride to blind him, and now he bore the physical and emotional scars of that mistake.

Chien ordered them to skin and butcher the tiger, a grim task that left the group silent and somber. Nhât worked beside Hung, his usual bravado replaced by quiet guilt. The shared burden of responsibility weighed heavily on both of them, though no words were exchanged.

As they worked through the night, Hung's mind turned over the events. The tiger had been a magnificent creature, reduced now to a lifeless carcass. It felt wrong, but he kept his hands moving, knowing the grisly work was a consequence of their actions.

When the sun rose, the tiger's skin lay stretched out before them, a haunting reminder of the previous night's horror. Hung stared at it, the weight of Chien's lessons settling in his mind.

Chien approached, his voice softer but still firm. "It's not just about surviving," he said. "It's about understanding the consequences of your actions. Think before you act."

Hung nodded, the lesson imprinted deep within him. He had faced death and lived, but the experience had changed him. The throbbing pain in his ankle would serve as a constant reminder of how close he had come to losing everything.

The group packed up in silence, moving with a new sense of caution. The youthful invincibility that had once defined them was gone, replaced by a more somber understanding of the dangers they faced. Nhât, once so full of bravado, remained unusually quiet, his guilt a tangible presence between them.

As they reached the shore, Chien turned to address the group one last time. "You've learned more than survival skills here," he said. "You've learned about yourselves, about fear, and about courage. Remember these lessons. They might save your life one day."

Chien paused, and then, as the others walked ahead, he placed a hand on Hung's shoulder. His tone softened. "There's something you should know, Hung. In my time,

I've met many men who've had to face their fears in the darkest places. One of them was a man named Master Lee."

Hung's ears perked up at the mention of the name. "Master Lee?"

Chien nodded slowly. "He's a man who thrived in environments like this—where the rules of honor and discipline don't always apply. His methods are… different from mine. But sometimes, survival means thinking like a predator. Master Lee understood that."

Hung furrowed his brow, unsure of what Chien was implying, but there was a weight to his words that suggested they carried great importance. "Do you think I'll need to learn from him?"

"I hope not," Chien replied, his expression serious.

"But if you ever find yourself in a situation where the usual rules don't apply, remember what I've told you."

The conversation left Hung with more questions than answers, but the significance of Chien's words lingered in his mind. There was a weight to them that Hung couldn't shake, a sense that this knowledge would be vital someday, even if he didn't yet understand how.

As they reached the canoe, the sun was just beginning to rise, casting long shadows across the beach. Hung limped slightly as they loaded the tiger's skin, its weight a physical reminder of the night's events. The other children moved more cautiously now, their youthful exuberance dulled by the lessons they had learned on the island.

Nhât walked beside Hung, unusually quiet. There was no need for words between them; the shared experience of the previous night had forged an unspoken understanding. Both of them had grown, their reckless bravado tempered by the raw reality of survival.

Chien stood at the shore, his eyes scanning the horizon before he turned to address the group one last time. His voice was firm but not unkind. "You've learned much during your time here, more than just how to survive.

You've learned about yourselves, about fear, and about courage. Remember these lessons. They will serve you well in life."

Hung watched as Chien's gaze softened slightly, lingering on each of them before finally resting on him.

There was a quiet pride in the way Chien looked at him, and for the first time, Hung felt as though he had earned it—not through feats of strength or daring, but through understanding.

As they paddled away from the island, the jungle slowly receded from view, its mysteries and dangers fading into the distance. But the lessons it had imparted—those would stay with Hung forever. He had faced death and survived, but more importantly, he had learned the true meaning of courage. It wasn't about the absence of fear, but the mastery of it. Every decision, every action, carried weight and consequences, and from now on, Hung would carry that understanding with him wherever life took him.

The journey back was silent, the sound of paddles cutting through the water the only noise as the island disappeared into the morning mist. Hung's ankle throbbed with pain, a constant reminder of the night's trials, but in his heart, he felt stronger—wiser.

Chien had taught him many things, but perhaps the most important lesson was that survival wasn't just about strength or skill. It was about knowing yourself, understanding your limitations, and having the wisdom to think before you act.

As they neared the mainland, Hung looked out across the water, the weight of Chien's words about Master Lee still heavy on his mind. He didn't know what the future held, but he knew he would carry the lessons of the jungle with him—lessons that might one day save his life.

CHAPTER 26

WAVES OF BRAVERY

"Bravery is being the only one who knows you're afraid." — Franklin P. Jones

The sun sank lower over the horizon, casting a soft golden glow across the sea, while the island they'd left behind faded into the distance. The scene appeared tranquil, but the memory of the crates they'd loaded—brimming with guns, ammunition, and explosives—lingered heavily on their minds. Each box had been a reminder of the dangerous mission ahead.

Hung leaned against the boat's railing, his fingers gripping the rough edge as his muscles still ached from the strenuous task of loading the ship hours before. The air was cooler now, but the tension among the crew was palpable. Tactical Training (TT) had demanded more than just physical endurance today—it required focus, relentless perseverance, and control.

From the deck of the boat, Chien watched in silence. His sharp eyes never left Hung, tracking every movement. Hung could feel the weight of that gaze, and when their eyes met, Chien offered a small, approving nod. It wasn't much, but it sent a surge of satisfaction through Hung.

His worth wasn't measured by words, but by action, and he was proving himself with every step.

At last, the final crate was loaded onto the boat. The sky had darkened, and the stars were beginning to dot the vast expanse above them. Hung collapsed momentarily against the boat, his breath coming in ragged gasps. His body was worn out, his muscles aching from the hours of labor. Yet, there was no time for weakness, no time for rest. The children around him stumbled toward their bunks, exhausted, but Hung's mind refused to quiet.

As he lay in his small bunk, staring at the wooden beams overhead, his thoughts raced. The island, the bomb, Chien's words—it all swirled in his mind, a chaotic blend of fear and excitement. This wasn't just about survival anymore; it was about proving himself. Proving he was worthy of Chien's trust. Every task, every lesson had been another step in his transformation. **Tactical Training (TT)** wasn't just physical—it was mental. The endurance to keep pushing, even when the body screamed to stop.

Chien stood at the bow of the boat, his gaze locked on the horizon. The sea was calm, mirroring the stillness of the sky above, but beneath that tranquility lurked an ever-present danger. His thoughts drifted as his fingers traced the smooth metal of a small silver cylinder. It was a habit, one that brought back memories he'd buried deep, but they resurfaced now as he stood alone.

The scent of saltwater and burning wood stirred something within him, pulling him back to a time long past, a time when he was no older than Hung.

Flashback: Chien's Past

It was the jungle—thick, humid, and alive with the sounds of war. Chien crouched low in the underbrush, his heart pounding in his chest as his hands worked quickly to assemble the bomb. His mentor, Minh, stood beside him, his face hardened by years of battle. The war had dragged on, and they were deep in the resistance, striking back at the enemy wherever they could. This was a mission—one that required precision and courage.

The jungle around them buzzed with life, but for Chien, there was only the bomb in his hands. His fingers moved deftly over the makeshift parts—scavenged metal, powder, wires, and a crude detonator. Minh's voice was low and steady as he guided him.

"Control the power, Chien," Minh had said, his voice carrying the weight of experience. "This isn't just about destruction. It's about sending a message. You must harness the chaos."

Chien's hands shook, but he kept working. They were setting a trap for an enemy convoy. The bomb had to be perfect—not too powerful, or it would blow the road apart and miss its target. Not too weak, or it would be nothing more than a warning. His mentor's words echoed in his mind as the minutes ticked by: control, precision, purpose.

Finally, the bomb was ready. Minh gave a curt nod of approval. "You've done well," he said. "Now, we wait."

The ambush had been successful. The bomb exploded with perfect timing, sending the enemy scattering, just as planned. Chien would never forget the rush of adrenaline as the explosion rocked the jungle—the shockwave rippling through the trees, the deafening roar that followed.

But what stayed with him most wasn't the destruction. It was Minh's words. Power wasn't just in the blast. It was in the control. The precision. The careful crafting of something deadly.

Back on the boat, Chien blinked, snapping back to the present as the crackling of the fire pulled him from his memories. His hands, now steady, worked the same way they had back in the jungle. The molten brick in front of him simmered in the steel pan, the smell of burning wood mixing with the salty air. The children had gathered around him, watching in silence as he worked.

Hung, standing at a distance, watched with rapt attention. He had seen Chien work before, but there was something different about tonight. Something heavier in the air. He could sense the importance of the moment, though he didn't know what memories were playing out behind Chien's calm expression.

Chien stirred the molten liquid, his hands moving with the practiced precision that came from years of experience. His mind remained sharp, the lessons of the past never far from his thoughts. Each bomb he crafted now was a reminder of that time in the jungle, of the delicate line between control and chaos.

"Hung," Chien called out suddenly, his voice cutting through the quiet. "Do we still have the rest of the cylinders?"

Hung snapped to attention, retrieving the backpack Nhât had carried. His hands trembled slightly as he passed it to Chien. This was another test, another moment where he had to prove himself. He stood silently, watching as Chien began to assemble the bomb with meticulous care.

"I've made bombs before," Hung said softly, almost to himself. "But those… they weren't like this."

Chien gave him a sideways glance, a faint smile tugging at his lips. "Messy bombs," he said, his tone calm. "They're made to destroy. This is different."

As the bomb took shape in Chien's hands, Hung could feel the weight of what was happening. This wasn't just about building a weapon. It was about control—about harnessing power with purpose. Every movement Chien made was deliberate, each step in the process a lesson in precision. This was **Knowledge Transfer (KT)** in its most vital form, passed down from master to student, from one generation to the next.

"This is a concussion bomb," Chien explained, holding up the device for the children to see. "It won't tear things apart. It sends out a shockwave—controlled, precise. It stuns, but it doesn't destroy."

The gravity of Chien's words hung in the air as the children watched in silence. The power of the bomb wasn't in its ability to kill, but in its ability to control. That was the lesson Chien had learned long ago in the jungle, and it was the lesson he was passing on now.

The canoe glided silently through the water, the moonlight reflecting off the calm surface as they paddled toward the drop site. Hung's heart raced in his chest, every stroke of the paddle deliberate. Beneath the surface, the water teemed with life, unaware of the force about to be unleashed.

Chien lowered the bomb into the water with slow, steady hands. "Move back," he whispered, and they paddled away, the tension thick in the air.

For a moment, there was silence. Then, the water erupted in a deep, resonating *boom*. The shockwave rippled outward, sending bubbles and debris shooting to the surface. The canoe rocked violently, and Sen let out a startled yelp as they fought to steady the boat.

But it didn't capsize.

Chien let out a low chuckle, his usually stern face breaking into a smile. "That worked better than I expected."

Hung peered over the edge of the canoe, his breath catching as he saw the fish floating to the surface.

Hundreds of them, intact. The nets went out, and in minutes, they had pulled a pile of fish, crabs, and even a small shark into the boat.

By the time they returned to the main vessel, the children were exhausted but triumphant. The day's work was done, and they had succeeded.

Later that night, as the boat swayed gently on the calm sea, Chien pulled Hung aside. His voice was soft but filled with pride.

"Little Dragon," he said, resting a hand on Hung's shoulder. "You've shown more bravery than most men I've known. Keep following your passion, and you'll always find your way."

Hung felt his chest swell with pride, the weight of Chien's words sinking in. As the boat sailed further into the distance, leaving the island behind, Hung stood at the bow, his eyes fixed on the horizon. The fear that had once held him back was still there, but it no longer controlled him. He had learned something far more valuable—control over his fear, over his power.

He wasn't the same boy who had stepped onto this boat. He was stronger now, wiser. And like Chien in the jungle, he understood the delicate balance between chaos and control. Whatever lay ahead, Hung knew he would face it with courage.

CHAPTER 27

STORMS WITHIN AND WITHOUT

"Life isn't about waiting for the storm to pass... It's about learning to dance in the rain." — Vivian Greene

Morning on High Tides:

The dawn arrived with an unsettling stillness. The sea, often lively with movement and sound, now lay perfectly still beneath a sky so clear it felt unnatural. The crew moved about the deck with practiced efficiency, but an air of unease lingered over them as the ship, *High Tides*, glided through the glassy water. Chien stood at the helm, his experienced eyes scanning the horizon. His instincts told him that this calm would not last. Nature, it seemed, was holding its breath.

After the morning chores, Chien steered the ship out of the sheltered cove, heading toward the mainland.

Their destination was a small port, a familiar stop where they could restock supplies and repair the ship after their recent skirmishes.

Hung sat beside Sen, who patiently guided him through his reading lessons. His brow furrowed as he traced the letters Sen had scratched onto the parchment, muttering under his breath. "I don't see how this helps," he grumbled. "Shouldn't I be training to fight instead?"

Sen smiled at his frustration, her voice light as she replied, "There's more power in knowledge than you think, Hung. It's not just about strength."

Hung sighed but continued tracing the letters with more focus. The thrill of action still burned within him, but lately, something had shifted. Chien's constant lessons, the harsh reality of the world they lived in, and the responsibilities that now rested on his shoulders had started to change him. He was beginning to understand that there was strength in the mind, in knowledge, just as much as there was in his fists.

Chien watched from the helm, his sharp gaze softened by a rare smile. He had seen Hung grow—his reflexes sharp, his instincts honed—but more importantly, he had seen the boy's heart remain intact. Despite all the hardships, Hung still retained his humanity, his decency.

Chien valued that more than any other skill.

"Remember, Hung," Chien called out, his voice steady against the sound of the waves, "knowledge will guide you when all else fails."

Hung glanced up, nodding, though impatience flickered across his face. He understood Chien's words, but part of him still craved action—the rush of adrenaline, the battles that lay ahead. But something inside him knew that Chien was right. Strength alone would never be enough.

Storm Preparation:

As the sun climbed higher, the air grew thick and oppressive. The once clear sky darkened, and the smell of salt mixed with something more foreboding. Chien sensed the change before anyone else, his years at sea telling him what was coming.

"Prepare the ship for a storm," he ordered, his tone calm but firm. "Secure the sails, check the rigging, and inspect the hull. We need to be ready."

Hung rose to his feet, his muscles tensing in anticipation. The crew moved quickly, their movements swift and coordinated as they prepared for the impending storm. But as always, Chien turned this moment of urgency into a lesson.

"This isn't just about following orders," Chien said as they worked. "It's about understanding why these tasks matter. Every action we take now could be the difference between surviving this storm and being at its mercy."

Hung listened carefully, his hands steady as he secured the ropes. He had always relied on his quick reflexes to navigate danger, but this was different. Chien was teaching him to think ahead, to anticipate, to plan.

This kind of tactical thinking required patience— something Hung had never been good at. But as he worked, a new sense of responsibility settled over him.

With each knot tied, with each command Chien gave, Hung felt the weight of leadership pressing down on him.

Chien's trust was both an honor and a burden. Hung was no longer just a boy trying to survive—he was learning to become a protector, someone others could rely on.

Trouble in Town:

When they reached the small port, the sky was dark, and the air carried a sense of impending doom. The crew disembarked, unloading the cargo with the efficiency of a well-practiced team. Chien slipped away into the town, his business private and quick, while Hung and Sen were sent to the market to pick up bread.

The marketplace was alive with color and noise, a stark contrast to the somber mood that had settled over the ship. Merchants called out their wares, and the air was thick with the scent of fresh bread and spices. Hung felt a brief moment of relief as he walked through the market, his senses overwhelmed by the vibrancy of it all.

As they weaved through the crowd, Sen's attention was drawn to a colorful scarf hanging in a stall. She reached out to touch it, her fingers brushing the fabric before the merchant shooed her away. She laughed, her voice light and carefree—a sound that seemed so distant from the heaviness that usually surrounded them.

But the moment of distraction cost them. Sen accidentally bumped into an older boy, sending him stumbling back. Before she could apologize, the boy shoved her to the ground.

"Watch it, little girl," he sneered, his voice full of menace. "You owe me for that."

Hung's anger flared, and he stepped forward, his voice sharp and commanding. "Leave her alone."

The boy smirked, his eyes narrowing as two of his friends appeared at his side. "Oh, we've got a tough guy here," he taunted, stepping closer.

Hung positioned himself between Sen and the boys, his fists clenched, ready for a fight. The leader struck first, grabbing Hung by the shirt and throwing him to the ground. Hung landed hard, the impact knocking the breath out of him, but he was up in an instant, his body reacting faster than his mind.

With a swift punch, Hung connected with the boy's jaw, sending him staggering back. One of the others lunged at Hung, but his attack was sloppy. Hung dodged the swing, and the boy stumbled, crashing into a nearby stall.

But the leader was quicker than Hung expected. He struck Hung hard in the side of the head, sending him reeling. Hung's vision blurred as he fell to his knees, the world spinning around him.

Sen, seeing her friend in trouble, didn't hesitate. She rushed forward, delivering a solid punch to the leader's face. He laughed, wiping the blood from his lip, but his laughter died when a shadow loomed over him.

Chien had arrived.

Without a word, the boy backed off, motioning for his friends to follow. "You're lucky this time," he spat, his eyes flicking to Chien. "Next time, you won't be."

As the boys disappeared into the crowd, Hung and Sen stood side by side, their adrenaline still coursing through them. "Are you okay?" Hung asked, his voice softer now.

Sen nodded, though her hands trembled slightly. "I'm fine," she whispered. "But I'm glad Chien showed up."

Back on High Tides:

By the time they returned to the ship, the sky had grown darker still. Chien was waiting for them, a calm but knowing look in his eyes. He had seen everything. Bandages and tea were laid out on the table, a silent acknowledgment of the trouble they had encountered.

"You saw?" Sen asked, her voice a mix of anger and disbelief.

"I did," Chien replied, his tone calm. "And it went just as I expected."

Sen's face flushed with anger. "You planned this?"

"It was a test," Chien said simply. "And you both passed."

Hung sat down, wincing as Chien tended to his wounds. "Seems like I have a knack for getting into trouble," Hung muttered.

"That you do," Chien said with a chuckle. "But you also have a knack for getting out of it."

As he finished wrapping Hung's bandage, Chien's expression grew serious. "I'm proud of you, boy. You have the makings of a leader. And when the time comes, I'd be honored if you considered my daughter, Sen, as your wife."

Hung's heart skipped a beat. He glanced at Sen, who blushed deeply, looking down at her lap. The idea of a future with her—a life beyond the battles and the storms—was a new and unexpected thought. He grinned despite the ache in his head. "Yes, sir," he said quietly.

The Storm:

The afternoon passed quickly as they prepared for the storm. Dark clouds filled the sky, and the wind began to howl. Chien moved with precision, directing the crew as they secured the rigging and reinforced the moorings.

"We may be in for a typhoon," Chien warned, his voice low but steady.

The first flash of lightning lit up the sky, followed by a deafening clap of thunder. The storm had arrived in full force.

CHAPTER 28

WRATH OF THE STORM

*"The storm is a good opportunity for the
pine and the cypress to show their strength
and stability."* — Ho Chi Minh

The wind screamed, tearing through the sky like a beast set free, fierce and relentless. Dark clouds churned overhead, swirling with a fury that mirrored the chaos below. The world seemed to fold beneath the storm's wrath, as if nature herself sought to test their endurance. This was no ordinary storm. It was a living, breathing force of destruction, unpredictable and merciless. Hung could feel it—this was not just about survival; it was a trial of the spirit, a test of everything they had learned.

The ship lurched violently, signaling the storm's full assault. Chien reacted instinctively, his voice sharp and commanding. "Below deck, now!" His words barely pierced the howling wind, but the children didn't hesitate. Eyes wide with fear, they scrambled to obey. Hung felt his heart pounding as he hurried after the others, each step a fight to stay upright on the slick, rain-soaked deck. The rain hit his face like needles, sharp and unyielding, driven by the gale's fury.

Behind them, Chien slammed the hatch shut, sealing them inside the ship's wooden belly. The sound of the storm was muffled but still overwhelming, the ship groaning under the relentless onslaught. Each creak of the timbers was a reminder that *High Tides* was fighting, much like they were, to stay afloat. Hung gripped a nearby beam, his knuckles white, and tried to steady his breathing. Chien's voice, calm and certain, echoed in his mind: *Breathe. Focus. Stay calm.*

The ship rocked violently, rising on the crest of a massive wave before crashing down into a trough with bone-jarring force. Hung's muscles tensed as he braced for the next lurch, his mind racing. *This isn't just a storm. It's a war.* And they were at its mercy. The children were thrown against the walls with each violent pitch of the ship, their fear palpable in the dim light of the swaying oil lamp. Chien moved swiftly, securing ropes and straps along the bulkheads. "Hold on tight," he ordered, his voice steady despite the chaos. His calmness was their lifeline.

Hung obeyed, gripping the rope as if his life depended on it. The bulkheads—the ship's spine—were the only thing keeping them anchored as the storm threatened to tear them apart. He glanced at Chien, watching how his mentor moved with such precision and focus. *This is what strength looks like*, Hung thought, *not just the power to fight, but the ability to stay composed when everything is falling apart.*

Minutes stretched into hours as the storm raged on, the noise unrelenting—a cacophony of wind, rain, and the ship's protests against the fury. Each crash of a wave felt like a blow to their very souls, testing their resolve.

Hung's mind was a whirlwind, much like the storm outside. He tried to focus on what Chien had taught them, to keep fear at bay, but it was almost impossible. The storm wasn't just a physical trial—it was mental, a battle against their own fear.

Suddenly, a loud clang echoed through the cabin as a tin cup flew off a shelf, narrowly missing Hung's head before clattering to the floor. He ducked reflexively, his heart racing. *Everything in here could kill us.* The thought gripped him with a new intensity. The storm wasn't just about the wind or the rain. It was about the countless dangers lurking in every corner. Any object could become a weapon, a reminder that survival wasn't guaranteed.

The ship pitched again, harder this time. Sen let out a small sob, her frail body trembling. Kim, ever the protector, reached for her hand, squeezing it tight. "We'll be okay," he whispered, though his voice wavered. His own fear was evident, but he masked it for Sen's sake.

Hung could see the uncertainty in Kim's eyes, the doubt that mirrored his own.

Chien noticed their exchange and gave a reassuring nod. His calm demeanor was unwavering, even in the face of such chaos. *This is what he taught us,* Hung reminded himself. *Stay calm, no matter what. The storm will pass.*

Chien's presence was an anchor, a steady force in the midst of the turmoil. The storm wasn't just a test of their physical endurance—it was a test of everything Chien had taught them about resilience and mental strength.

Hung closed his eyes and focused on his breathing, forcing himself to block out the noise. He could feel the ship beneath him, creaking and straining, but holding strong. *You cannot control the storm, but you can control how you face it.* Chien's words echoed in his mind, grounding him. This storm, like every challenge they had faced, would pass. But it was the lessons learned that would endure.

Hours dragged on. The relentless motion of the ship, the cold, the damp, the fear—it all wore on them, slowly chipping away at their strength. Hung's muscles ached from bracing himself against the wall, but it was the constant tension, the waiting, that was the hardest to bear. His thoughts drifted back to the streets of his village, to the alleys where fear had always lurked, waiting to strike. *I survived that. I'll survive this.*

And then, slowly, the storm began to abate. The wind, still fierce, no longer screamed with the same intensity. The rain eased to a steady, rhythmic beat. The violent pitching of the ship calmed, though the occasional lurch kept them all on edge. Chien untied them, his face serious but calm. "We're not out of it yet," he warned. The children nodded, exhausted but alert.

Hung stood on shaky legs, his body aching with exhaustion. The adrenaline was wearing off, leaving behind a deep fatigue. But there was no time to rest.

Chien's voice, ever practical, brought them back to reality. "We need to assess the damage."

They followed him to the deck, climbing through the wreckage that had blocked the hatch. The wind still whipped at their faces, but it was nothing compared to the earlier fury. What they saw above was sobering. The deck was littered with debris, the once-sturdy deckhouse shattered. The windows of the bridge were broken, shards of glass glittering under the weak light. *High Tides* had survived, but only just.

Hung forced himself to look out over the harbor. The storm had left devastation in its wake. Other ships, less fortunate than theirs, lay capsized or sinking. Bodies floated among the wreckage, a grim reminder of the storm's deadly power. His stomach churned as he watched the rescue efforts. *How close had they come?*

Chien's voice snapped him back to the present. "Start clearing the deck. Salvage what you can." There was no time to dwell on the destruction. They had survived, and now they had to move forward. Hung, Kim, Sen, and the others worked with a quiet determination, their bodies weary but their resolve hardened. Each movement felt like an act of defiance, a refusal to be broken by the storm.

As they worked, Hung's thoughts turned inward. *This is the event that changes everything.* The storm had been a test, but it wasn't the end. It was the beginning, this storm had taught them something more than survival—it had shown them their true strength. And that strength would be needed for what lay ahead.

By the time the skies began to clear and the oppressive heat returned, they had managed to clear most of the deck. Their bodies were exhausted, but their spirits had not broken. Hung glanced at Chien, who stood silently, surveying the damage with calm eyes. His mentor's hands, usually so steady, bore the faint tremor of a man who had faced something monumental and come through the other side.

The sun began to set, casting a warm, golden glow over the battered harbor. For a brief moment, everything was still. The storm was over. They had survived. But the weight of what they had faced, and what was yet to come, lingered in the air.

Chien's voice, quiet but filled with pride, broke the silence. "We've done well today. Tomorrow, we rebuild." His words were not just about the ship. They were about them all—about how they would take what they had learned, the strength they had discovered, and use it to face whatever came next.

Hung looked out at the calm sea, the storm now a distant memory. But something inside him had shifted. The storm had tested them, pushed them to their limits, but it had also revealed something deeper. *This is the event that changes everything.* And in the silence that followed, he knew they were ready.

CHAPTER 29

REBUILDING AND RESILIENCE

"The human capacity for burden is like bamboo—far more flexible than you'd ever believe at first glance."—Jodi Picoult

Two weeks had passed since the typhoon had ravaged the **High Tides**, leaving it battered and broken. Now, under the relentless determination of Chien and the children, the vessel was slowly restored, plank by plank. The ship, once on the verge of collapse, stood resilient against the horizon, a testament to their perseverance. Every strike of the hammer echoed with more than just the sound of metal on wood—it was the beat of survival, the rhythm of rebuilding both the ship and themselves.

Chien stood at the bow, his keen eyes watching the children as they worked tirelessly. Each of them had taken to the tasks with unwavering focus, as if the storm had shifted something deep within them. The lessons Chien imparted carried more than the weight of instructions— they carried the weight of survival.

"Every repair," Chien said, his voice calm and steady like the waves that lapped against the hull, "is an investment in your future. Knowledge is like a tool—useless unless you know how to apply it."

The children nodded, absorbing every word. They weren't just fixing a ship anymore; they were learning how to fix themselves, their lives, and their futures. Every task, from mending sails to nailing down planks, carried the essence of the **KT3 principle** of **Knowledge Transfer (KT)**. They weren't just preparing the **High Tides** for the sea again—they were preparing themselves for the unknown storms that lay ahead.

Reflection:

Hung, his hands blistered from the constant labor, looked at Chien with a mixture of awe and determination.

The storm had tested every ounce of his strength, but it had also awakened something inside him. He wasn't the same scared boy who had cowered at the sight of danger. Each day of work, each lesson Chien shared, felt like a new layer of armor being forged around him.

His hands, though sore, were steady now, more skilled with every nail he hammered into the ship's frame.

"I never thought rebuilding could feel like this," Hung thought, his brow furrowed in concentration as he secured another plank. *"It's like every piece of wood we fix makes me stronger too."*

As the days passed, they began to feel a strange comfort in the routine of rebuilding. The rhythmic sound of tools hitting wood became a source of solace. Yet beneath the surface, there was an unsettling tension. Figures had started appearing at the edge of the quay—silent, shadowy figures that moved like ghosts through the mist. Chien noticed them first, and soon the children followed, their eyes wide with a mix of curiosity and unease.

Chien, always vigilant, had prepared them for this. He had drilled into them the importance of remaining alert, of always being aware of their surroundings—core principles of **Tactical Training (TT)**. The makeshift alarm system he'd devised—a string cord attached to a knife suspended in a glass jar in his cabin—became a constant reminder that danger was never far away.

"Stay sharp," Chien would say, his voice low and steady. "Not all knowledge is safe. Some secrets are best left undiscovered."

The children, though young, understood the weight of his words. Not every lesson could be learned in the light of day. Some knowledge was dangerous, and the men lurking near the harbor were proof of that. They watched, they waited, and the children knew better than to ask questions.

The air around the harbor was thick with humidity, the salty tang of the sea mixing with the smell of fresh wood and tar. Every morning, the mist would roll in, cloaking the ship and the harbor in a damp haze. The figures—silent, watchful—would stand at the edge of the quay, their outlines barely visible through the fog. The children felt their presence before they saw them, a cold shiver running down their spines whenever they glanced toward the shore.

Hung could hear the faint clink of metal in the distance, the sound of the men sharpening their knives or perhaps shifting their weapons. It sent a ripple of unease through him, but he forced himself to focus on his work. He had to trust Chien's judgment. They all did.

As the **High Tides** neared completion, the sense of accomplishment was palpable. The children had learned to barter for fish, negotiate for supplies, and repair the ship under Chien's watchful eye. Every task was a lesson in survival—one that extended beyond just rebuilding the ship.

One evening, as the sun began to dip below the horizon, casting long shadows across the deck, Chien gathered the children. His face was weathered, etched with the strain of the past few weeks, yet his eyes gleamed with the quiet intensity of someone who had seen too much.

"We've done well," he began, his voice steady but heavy with the weight of unspoken fears, "but remember, this is only the beginning. The storm taught us something important—always be prepared, always learn from what happens. Every repair, every negotiation—it's all part of your training. Next time, we'll be even quicker, even stronger."

The children nodded in agreement, their hearts swelling with pride. They had transformed in these two weeks, no longer just children—they were survivors, each lesson, each challenge forging their resilience. They had rebuilt the ship, but more importantly, they had rebuilt themselves.

Finally, the day came when the **High Tides** was ready to sail. Her hull still bore the scars of the typhoon, but it was those very scars that made her stronger, a testament to their hard work and perseverance. Chien, standing tall at the helm, gave the order to load the last of the supplies. The children, though weary, felt a renewed sense of purpose. Home was on the horizon.

As the ship glided through the calm waters, Hung leaned against the railing, watching the sea part beneath them. For the first time in weeks, he felt a moment of peace. The storm had passed, and the journey ahead, for now, seemed calm.

The sight of their home port stirred a mix of relief and anticipation in their hearts. The children rushed to unload the supplies, their eyes scanning the shoreline for signs of damage. The storm had been fierce, but the damage was minimal. They had survived. That night, Chien prepared a small feast, a celebration of their return.

The candlelight flickered in the warm night air as laughter echoed across the deck. For the first time in weeks, the tension broke, and the children felt free. Chien raised his cup, his voice carrying a note of pride as he declared, "To survival."

The children cheered, their spirits lightened by the moment, but the peace didn't last long.

The Pigman Returns:

Hung, tasked with fetching more wine from the market, strolled back toward the ship, bottle in hand. The marketplace, though quieter than usual, still buzzed with the remnants of the day's trade. The smell of roasted fish and herbs lingered in the air, mingling with the distant sound of waves crashing against the shore. For a moment, Hung allowed himself to relax, the weight of the past weeks slipping away.

But the peace was short-lived. A sudden jerk from behind yanked him off his feet, the bottle slipping from his grasp as he crashed to the ground. His heart pounded in his chest as he looked up, his vision blurry from the impact.

Standing over him, with a twisted grin and eyes gleaming with malice, was the Pigman.

"You've cost me, boy," the Pigman snarled, his voice low and menacing. "Now it's time to pay."

Panic surged through Hung as the Pigman's hand reached for him, his grip tightening like a vice around Hung's collar. The fight that followed was brutal, each blow from the Pigman sending pain coursing through Hung's body. He struggled to recall Chien's teachings— stay calm, find an opening—but the Pigman's brute force overwhelmed him. Every punch blurred his vision, and each breath felt like it might be his last.

Just as darkness threatened to take him, a shadow emerged from the alley—Chien.

In an instant, the air around them shifted. Chien moved with a deadly precision that made the Pigman seem slow and clumsy in comparison. With a few swift, calculated strikes, Chien disarmed him, his movements fluid and precise. Within moments, the Pigman was on his knees, gasping for breath, defeated.

Reflection:

Hung lay on the ground, his body aching and his mind reeling from the fight. As he watched Chien, a deep sense of awe and gratitude filled him. Chien had saved him—again. But more than that, he had shown him what true strength looked like. It wasn't about brute force; it was about control, precision, and discipline—the very heart of **Tactical Training (TT)**.

Chien knelt beside him, his face drawn with concern. Without a word, he scooped Hung into his arms and hurried back to the ship. Fear gnawed at Chien's insides in a way it never had before. The principles of Tactical Training had saved Hung, but Chien couldn't shake the feeling that the danger was far from over.

CHAPTER 30

REST AND RECOVERY

"The greatest glory in living lies not in never falling, but in rising every time we fall."—Nelson Mandela

Chien sat in the hospital waiting room, his mind churning with a relentless mix of emotions. The events of the past few hours replayed in his head like an endless loop: the vicious fight with the Pigman, the sound of Hung's body hitting the ground, the desperate race to the hospital. Now, surrounded by the sterile white walls, the coldness seemed to amplify the weight pressing on his chest. The steady hum of hospital equipment was a harsh reminder that Hung's life still hung in the balance.

Each tick of the wall clock felt like a hammer blow, each second dragging on unbearably. His children sat nearby, their faces pale, their eyes distant. They had retreated into their own thoughts, too exhausted and afraid to speak. The silence between them was suffocating, like a heavy blanket of dread.

The door creaked open, the sound shattering the stillness. Chien's heart leapt in his chest as he stood, every muscle in his body tense as the doctor stepped into the room. Time slowed, the air thick with unspoken fear.

"Hung is stable," the doctor said, his voice calm, measured. "He suffered a severe concussion, and there's some swelling on his brain. We're monitoring it closely. If all goes well, the swelling should subside in a few days."

The words washed over Chien like a gust of cold wind. Relief surged through him, nearly overwhelming his senses. His knees wobbled slightly as the tension that had been gripping him for hours began to ease. *Hung is stable*, he repeated silently, holding onto the words like a lifeline. Still, the knot of worry in his chest remained.

The doctor continued, "He'll need to stay here for a few days, just to be safe. But for now, go home and rest. There's nothing more you can do tonight."

Chien nodded, though the thought of leaving Hung alone in the hospital gnawed at him. Yet, the doctor was right—there was nothing more he could do. With a heavy heart, he gathered the children and led them back to the **High Tides**, the ship resting quietly in the nearby harbor.

On Board the High Tides:

The walk back to the ship was silent, the sound of their footsteps swallowed by the night. Only the rhythmic lapping of the waves against the hull broke the stillness.

Once aboard, Chien assigned each of the children a task—something to keep their hands busy, something to pull their minds away from the fear that still gripped them. He had used this strategy before, during the hardest of times. It wasn't a solution, but it helped.

Kim, the oldest, took to stitching the sails. His hands moved with a practiced precision, pulling the thread through the fabric with steady motions. Every stitch felt like a prayer, each knot tied with care. His gaze occasionally lifted to the sky, where the moon hung low and bright, casting a silver light over the water. *I hope Hung can see the moon too,* Kim thought, wishing his brother could draw some comfort from the same light.

Nhât scrubbed the deck, his usual energy replaced by a quiet, grim focus. he moved methodically, he brush sweeping back and forth in long strokes. But no matter how hard he scrubbed, the image of Hung lying pale and still clung to he like a shadow he couldn't shake.

Sen, the youngest, sat with a fishing net, her small hands carefully weaving the frayed threads back together.

Every knot she tied felt like an act of defiance against the fear threatening to swallow her whole. *If I can fix this net, maybe I can help fix Hung too,* she thought, her hands moving with determined purpose.

As the night wore on, they gathered in the galley for a simple meal. The usual laughter and light banter were absent, replaced by a heavy silence. The air in the room felt thick, oppressive, as if it were weighing them down.

Chien watched his children, his heart aching. They were too young to carry such heavy burdens, yet here they were, stronger than most adults he had known.

Sleep, when it finally came, was elusive. The gentle rocking of the boat, which usually brought them comfort, did little to soothe their troubled minds. The sound of the boat creaking in the night only served as a reminder of the dangers they faced—dangers they were only just beginning to understand.

The Next Morning:

Chien rose at dawn, his body moving automatically through the familiar routine of preparing for the day. He packed a few essentials into his satchel, readying himself to return to the hospital. As he passed by the children's cabins, he was surprised to find them already awake, standing quietly in a line. Their faces, though tired, were set with determination.

A surge of pride welled up in Chien's chest. The children had grown so much, molded by the challenges they had faced together. Without a word, he nodded, acknowledging their silent resolve. "Let's go," he said simply, his voice steady as he released the mooring lines and prepared the boat for the short sail back to the hospital.

The journey was quiet, the tension clinging to them like a heavy fog. Each of them was lost in their own thoughts, their fears and hopes swirling together. Chien kept his gaze fixed on the horizon, repeating the doctor's words in his mind: *Hung is stable. He's going to be fine.*

At the Hospital:

When they arrived at the hospital, they hurried inside, their hearts pounding with anticipation. The nurse directed them to a waiting area, and within minutes, the doctor appeared, his face lit up with a broad smile.

"How is he?" Chien asked, his voice a mix of hope and apprehension.

The doctor chuckled softly. "Hung woke up last night and hasn't stopped eating since. We had to bring in extra food just to keep up with him!"

Relief flooded through Chien, nearly bringing him to his knees. The children burst into laughter, their joy filling the sterile halls and washing away the fear that had lingered for days.

"He'll need to stay another day or two for observation," the doctor continued, "but you can see him now."

Without waiting for more, the children raced down the hallway, their footsteps light and full of excitement. Chien followed at a more measured pace, though his heart raced with anticipation. When they entered Hung's room, his face lit up with a grin.

"Careful with the bump," Hung joked, though he winced slightly. "It's still a bit sore."

Chien stood back, watching as the children gathered around Hung, their faces beaming with joy and relief. Hung's strength had always been physical, but now Chien saw something deeper—an inner resilience, a strength that had been forged through hardship.

The Healer's Wisdom:

As the room filled with laughter and chatter, the door creaked open, and a nurse entered, carrying a tray of tea and herbs. Her presence was calming, her movements graceful and deliberate. She smiled at Hung and offered him a cup of tea.

"This will help ease the pain," she said softly. "And I have something more to show you."

Hung, curious, accepted the tea and took a sip, feeling the warmth spread through his body. The nurse, who introduced herself as Master Linh, began guiding him through a series of breathing exercises, her voice calm and steady as she explained the flow of energy—chi—and how it could be harnessed for healing.

Chien, standing quietly in the corner, stiffened when he heard the name. Recognition flickered in his eyes as he looked at the nurse more closely. "Master Linh?"

The nurse—Master Linh—turned and smiled warmly.

"It's been a long time, Chien. I see you've become quite the protector."

Chien nodded, a quiet respect in his voice. "And you still heal."

Master Linh returned her gaze to Hung. "You are strong," she said, her voice filled with gentle encouragement. "But strength is not just in the body. You have much to learn, and the road ahead will not be easy. But I see you have the strength to walk it."

Hung listened intently, feeling something shift inside him. There was more to this than simple recovery—this was the beginning of something deeper, a journey he had not yet fully understood. And though the path ahead was uncertain, he felt a growing sense of determination.

As the day drew to a close, Chien bowed deeply to Master Linh. "We'll be back tomorrow," he said, his voice filled with gratitude.

CHAPTER 31

A GROWING FEAR

"Change is the end result of all true learning." — Leo Buscaglia

The first light of dawn filtered through the cracks in the cabin walls, casting a soft glow over Chien's weathered face. He sat upright on his bed, his thoughts already swirling with the weight of the day ahead. The cool morning breeze seeped through the wooden slats, a familiar comfort that usually brought him peace.

But today, the breeze did little to ease the tension coiling in his chest.

Hung's future, the boy he had come to love as his own, now seemed uncertain. The cost of his recovery weighed heavily on Chien's mind, gnawing at his every thought. The doctor had reassured him that Hung was healing well, but Chien knew they couldn't afford much longer at the hospital. As much as Chien tried to stay hopeful, a nagging sense of dread crept into his heart.

A Heavy Breakfast:

The children gathered on deck for breakfast, their voices bubbling with excitement. Today was a special day—they were going to visit Hung at the hospital and bring him home. The kids' joy and innocent chatter filled the air, but for Chien, every bite of food felt like it might choke him. His stomach was in knots. He watched them smile, laugh, and talk about their reunion with Hung, yet his thoughts remained dark, clouded by uncertainty.

How could he explain to them what was happening? He had rehearsed the conversation in his mind a dozen times, but each attempt felt inadequate. The truth was, he didn't know what the future held for Hung—how they would pay for the treatment or whether Hung could stay with them. And no matter how much he prepared himself for the decisions ahead, the fear of what could happen gnawed at his resolve.

Chien cleared his throat as he finished his meal, signaling to the children that it was time to leave. They jumped to their feet, eager to set off. Each step they took toward the hospital seemed heavier than the last for Chien. His mind was consumed with worries about how they would cover Hung's medical bills, and whether they would be able to keep the boy in their care.

The Walk to the Hospital:

The sun rose higher in the sky as they made their way through the winding streets of the town. The children skipped ahead, their laughter echoing through the quiet morning. Chien followed slowly behind, his feet dragging with each step. He knew that this might be the last day of their lives as they knew it. The children were blissfully unaware of the storm that loomed on the horizon. For them, it was just another day—a happy day, in fact— because they were going to see Hung.

As they approached the hospital, the building loomed ahead, its white walls bathed in the warm glow of the rising sun. Chien's heart pounded in his chest as they reached the entrance. The children rushed ahead, their excitement palpable, but Chien hesitated at the door. He took a deep breath, trying to steady himself. He wasn't ready for what might come next.

Inside, they found Hung waiting near the front desk. His face lit up when he saw them, and despite the fading bruises, there was a joy in his eyes that made Chien's heart ache. The children rushed to him, enveloping him in a tight embrace, their laughter filling the sterile space of the hospital. For a moment, everything felt right. For a moment, Chien allowed himself to believe that this happiness could last.

But he knew better.

The Unsettling Truth:

As the children chatted excitedly with Hung, the doctor approached Chien with a smile. "Hung's healing well," he said after checking the boy's vitals one last time.

"He's ready to go home, though he'll need to rest for a few more days."

Chien nodded, grateful but distracted. His mind was elsewhere—on the conversation he needed to have, on the cost of Hung's treatment. As the children gathered Hung's things and prepared to leave, Chien lingered behind. His heart raced as he approached the doctor, his mouth dry.

"Doctor," Chien began, his voice unsteady, "I don't have much money for Hung's treatment, but I'll give you everything I have."

The doctor's response came swiftly, catching Chien off guard. "There's no need to worry about payment. A gentleman came by late last night and settled the bill."

Chien blinked, confusion momentarily clouding his thoughts. "Who?"

The doctor's expression softened. "He said he was Hung's uncle."

The words hit Chien like a blow to the chest. His stomach dropped, and his breath caught in his throat.

Hung's uncle. The man had come, just as Chien had feared, and had found them.

The doctor continued, unaware of the turmoil now raging inside Chien. "He said he would return this morning to meet you."

Chien nodded numbly, unable to respond. His mind raced. The reality of the situation—the possibility of losing Hung—sank in deeper with every second. He thanked the doctor quietly before turning to rejoin the children.

A Somber Walk Back:

Chien trailed behind the children as they made their way back from the hospital. His worst fears were coming true. Hung's family had found him, and now the boy might be taken away. The thought of losing him—to people who had abandoned him long ago—was almost unbearable.

The children chattered happily, oblivious to the storm brewing inside Chien. They gathered around Hung, their laughter filling the air, but the joy that had filled the morning was gone for Chien, replaced by a hollow ache in his chest.

As they reached the boat, Hung looked up at Chien, his smile fading as he sensed the shift in mood. "Sir? Why aren't we heading back yet?"

Chien hesitated, then slowly walked over to where the children sat. The air around them grew tense, and the smiles vanished from their faces as they noticed Chien's serious expression.

"I spoke to the doctor," Chien said, his voice heavy with the weight of the news. "He told me something I didn't expect. When I went to pay for Hung's treatment, the doctor told me the bill had already been covered."

Hung's brow furrowed, and the children glanced between each other in confusion.

"The doctor said it was your uncle who paid," Chien added quietly.

Hung's face fell, the joy draining from his expression.

The other children looked at him, worry filling their young eyes. Chien could feel the tension rise, the unspoken questions hanging in the air.

"Where is he now?" Hung asked, his voice barely above a whisper.

"He'll be coming back," Chien said, trying to keep his voice steady. "He wants to see you."

Hung swallowed hard, lowering his gaze. "I thought... I thought they didn't want me anymore."

Chien's heart broke at the boy's words. He knelt down beside Hung, placing a hand on his shoulder. "You're never a burden, Hung," he said softly. "And no matter what happens, you'll always be part of this family."

Hung nodded slowly, his hands resting in his lap as he tried to process the news. The thought of seeing his family again, after all these years, stirred a complex mix of emotions in the boy's heart—fear, anger, and a strange longing for the past he had left behind.

The Uncle's Arrival:

As the sun dipped lower in the sky, Chien glanced toward the shore. In the distance, he saw a man approaching. His stride was purposeful, and his eyes scanned the boat as he drew near. Chien's heart sank.

The moment he had dreaded was here.

"Hung," Chien said quietly, his voice strained. "Is that your uncle?"

Hung glanced up, his expression tight with tension. "Yes, sir," he replied softly, his voice barely a whisper.

The children, sensing the change in the air, fell silent. They gathered closer to Hung, their faces filled with concern. Chien stood and looked at them for a moment before making a decision.

"Go below deck for now," he instructed gently.

The children hesitated, exchanging worried glances with Hung, but they obeyed, slipping below deck just as the man reached the boat.

Chien turned toward the approaching figure, steeling himself. The man's gaze locked onto Hung as he stepped onto the boat, and the weight of the moment pressed heavily on Chien's chest.

CHAPTER 32

THE CROSSROADS OF FAMILY

"Family is not an important thing. It's everything." — Michael J. Fox

The morning sun climbed higher into the sky as the man stepped aboard the boat. Chien stood still, his body tense with anticipation. The man's eyes scanned the deck, finally resting on Hung, who sat quietly at the table. The children had gone below deck, leaving the space heavy with unspoken tension. Chien's heart pounded in his chest as he realized that this moment—the one he had feared—had arrived. Hung's uncle had come.

The man approached, his footsteps echoing faintly on the wooden planks. Chien stepped forward, offering a hand. "You must be Hung's uncle."

The man nodded, shaking Chien's hand firmly. "I am," he replied, his gaze shifting quickly to Hung. "I've been looking for him for a long time."

Chien's chest tightened. He swallowed, struggling to find the right words. He had known this day might come, but now that it was here, he felt unprepared.

Hung remained seated, his face a mask of composure, but Chien could sense the storm of emotions brewing beneath the surface. He had seen the boy grow from a frightened, malnourished child into a resilient young man. And now, Hung's past had caught up with him.

"Hung," his uncle said softly, stepping closer. "Your mother has been worried sick. She wants you to come home. She's been waiting for you."

Hung's eyes flickered with emotion, but he remained silent, staring down at the table. Chien felt his heart break a little as he watched the boy wrestle with the decision before him. The family that had seemingly abandoned him had returned, but what did that mean now? Could he trust them? Could he leave behind the life he had built with Chien and the other children?

Chien stepped forward, placing a hand on Hung's shoulder. "Take your time," he said gently, his voice steady despite the turmoil churning in his chest. "This isn't an easy decision."

Hung looked up at him, his eyes glassy with unshed tears. "I don't know what to do, sir," he whispered.

Chien knelt beside the boy, keeping his voice low and calm. "Whatever you decide, you're not alone. You have a family here with us. But you also have a family that's been searching for you. You need to decide where your heart belongs."

Hung's uncle, sensing the gravity of the moment, remained silent, giving the boy space to process the situation. Chien was grateful for that. He knew how overwhelming this must be for Hung—a boy who had felt abandoned for so long was now faced with the chance to reunite with his family.

Hung's hands trembled slightly as he gripped the edge of the table. He had thought of his family often during the long nights he spent alone before meeting Chien, but those thoughts had always been tainted by the pain of feeling unwanted. Now, faced with the reality of his uncle standing before him, Hung didn't know what to believe.

"I thought they didn't want me," Hung said quietly, his voice barely audible. "I thought I was a burden to them."

Chien's heart ached at the boy's words. He had always sensed that deep down, Hung carried a wound that no amount of physical training could heal—a wound left by abandonment, by the belief that he wasn't good enough.

"You're not a burden, Hung," Chien said softly, his voice thick with emotion. "You've never been a burden. Not to me, and not to them."

Hung's uncle stepped forward, his expression earnest.

"We never stopped looking for you, Hung. I know it may not seem like it, but your mother has been trying to find you for years. She's never given up hope."

Hung's gaze remained fixed on the floor, his mind clearly racing with conflicting emotions. Chien could see the pain and confusion in his eyes. It was the same look he had seen in countless children over the years—those who had been abandoned, neglected, or left to fend for themselves. And yet, this was different. Hung wasn't being asked to survive on his own anymore. He was being asked to choose between two families.

Chien stood and took a step back, giving Hung the space he needed. He knew that this decision had to come from the boy's heart. No amount of advice or persuasion from him would change that. All he could do was be there for him, no matter what he chose.

"Hung," Chien said softly, "whatever happens, you'll always be a part of this family. You've grown so much, and you've learned things that will stay with you for the rest of your life. But now, you have a chance to reconnect with your past. You have the chance to go home."

Hung's eyes finally met his uncle's. The man's expression was filled with hope and longing, but there was also a hint of fear—fear that Hung might reject him, might choose to stay with Chien and the life he had built here. The tension in the air was thick, as if the entire world was holding its breath, waiting for Hung's decision.

"I…" Hung began, his voice shaky. He looked back at Chien, then at his uncle. "I need some time. I need to think."

His uncle nodded, understanding. "Take all the time you need, Hung. I'll return home and let your mother know you're safe. When you're ready, come home. We'll be waiting for you."

With that, the man gave Hung a final, reassuring smile, then turned and stepped off the boat, leaving him with Chien and the children to say their goodbyes.

The Heart of a Family:

As the sun began to set, casting a golden glow over the harbor, the children emerged from below deck, sensing that the mood had shifted. They gathered around Hung, their faces filled with concern, but also with love.

They didn't need to know all the details to understand that something important was happening. They simply wanted to be there for their friend.

Chien watched as Hung interacted with the other children, the weight of the decision still heavy on his shoulders. He could see the bond they had formed— the family they had built together, not through blood, but through shared experiences, trust, and love. It was this bond that made the decision so difficult for Hung. He had found a home here, a place where he belonged. But now, the past was pulling him in another direction.

"Hung," Chien said gently, breaking the silence. "No matter what you decide, this is your family too. And no matter where you go, you'll never be alone."

Hung nodded, his eyes filled with gratitude. He knew that Chien was right. He wasn't alone—not anymore.

With a deep breath, Hung stood. The weight of the decision still hung over him, but there was a new resolve in his eyes. He walked over to the children, who had gathered around him, eyes shimmering with emotion.

The Final Goodbye:

The children crowded around Hung, their eyes brimming with unshed tears. They hugged him tightly, and he returned each embrace, whispering promises to visit, to write, to never forget them. It was a bittersweet moment, filled with both joy and sorrow. As the children's laughter faded into gentle whispers of goodbye, Hung felt the depth of their bond—one that transcended blood.

Chien watched quietly from the side, his heart heavy yet full of pride. He had known this day would come—the day when Hung would choose his own path. And though it hurt to let him go, Chien knew that this wasn't truly goodbye. Their bond was unbreakable.

Hung approached Chien, the two standing face to face. "I'll come back to visit," Hung promised, his voice steady despite the emotion behind it.

Chien nodded, swallowing the lump in his throat. "You'll always have a place here, Hung."

As the last light of the sun slipped below the horizon, Hung took one last look at the family he had grown with. His eyes glistened, and with a final wave, he stepped off the boat.

CHAPTER 33

FINAL FAREWELLS

*"Every new beginning comes from some
other beginning's end." — Seneca*

The sun hung low in the sky, casting long shadows over the dirt road as Hung walked toward the village.

The weight of the water buckets on his shoulders felt almost nonexistent compared to the heaviness lodged deep in his chest. Each step stirred up a cloud of dust, and with it, memories that had been buried in the corners of his mind. Chien, Kim, Sen, Nhât—the family he had forged at sea—each face flickered in his thoughts, and each name stung like salt on an open wound. Nine months on the High Tides had transformed him in ways deeper than he ever thought possible. Yet, as the silhouette of his village grew sharper on the horizon, doubts crept back into his heart, clawing at him like shadows reaching out from the past.

The village stood unchanged, as though time itself had forgotten this corner of the world. The same crooked trees lined the fields, the same rooftops sagged under years of neglect. But Hung was no longer the same boy who had left this place. His body had grown stronger, his mind sharper, his spirit tempered like steel under pressure. And yet, each step toward home felt like walking backward into the past—a past he had fought so hard to leave behind.

As he neared the village well, a vivid memory crashed over him like a wave against the shore. The first time he had trudged along this road, his body beaten and his soul bruised, fetching water for Chien. That memory had been fueled by anger and fear. But now, after everything, those feelings had been replaced with something else— something stronger, yet more elusive. Was it resolve? Or was it the residue of fear, still clinging to him, a fear that his past would rise up and pull him under once more?

His muscles burned as he climbed the hill toward home, but the ache in his heart outweighed the physical strain. He hoisted the buckets higher on his shoulders, the water sloshing inside. He could still feel the weight of Chien's farewell that morning—the stoic look in his mentor's eyes, masking the sadness beneath. The children had clung to him, their small hands grasping at his shirt as tears soaked through the fabric. He had forced himself to remain composed, but now, alone on this road, the emotions hit him in waves—grief, longing, and an aching sense of finality.

The road was unchanged, but Hung was seeing it through new eyes. The trees that once seemed so tall now felt insignificant after the vastness of the ocean. The village, which had been his entire world, now felt like a cage—a cage he knew he had to step back into if he was ever to truly leave it behind.

As the village crept closer, his pace slowed. Familiar landmarks—the tree he used to climb, the fields where his mother toiled—brought pangs of nostalgia, but they also stirred darker memories. He had changed, but had the village? Had his mother? Would he still fit into this world, or had he outgrown it, becoming a stranger to the life he once knew?

A voice, deep and mocking, shattered his thoughts.

"You're fetching me water again. That's good."

Hung's heart skipped a beat, and he froze. He knew that voice. Turning slowly, he saw three boys step out from the shadows, their broad shoulders and cruel grins unmistakable. These were the village bullies, a reminder of the life he had fought so hard to escape. The leader, a hulking figure with a crooked smile, stood at the front, his eyes gleaming with malice.

"How kind of him," one of the others sneered, his voice dripping with sarcasm.

"We should thank him properly," the third added with a chuckle, his icy tone sending a shiver down Hung's spine.

Fear clawed at Hung's chest, a familiar sensation, but this time, something was different. Beneath the fear, a calmness settled. His mind cleared, no longer fogged by panic. He assessed the situation quickly—the open road behind him, no obstacles, no hidden dangers. He had choices. He could act.

In an instant, Hung made his decision.

Without a word, he gripped the wooden staff that held the buckets and swung it with all the strength he had. The first bucket shattered as it collided with the leader's face, splinters of wood and water flying through the air. The other two boys froze, stunned by the suddenness of the attack. Hung didn't hesitate. In one fluid motion, he spun, using the momentum to send the second bucket hurtling toward the nearest boy. It smashed into his knee with a sickening crack, and he crumpled to the ground, howling in pain.

The third boy, wide-eyed and desperate, fumbled for a rock. He hurled it at Hung, the jagged stone catching him in the back with a thud. The impact knocked Hung off his feet, the wind rushing from his lungs as he hit the dirt. His mouth filled with the metallic taste of blood as he gasped for air. His vision blurred, but his mind remained focused—survival was all that mattered now.

Before Hung could regain his footing, the leader, bleeding from his face, wrenched the staff from his grip and swung it down at him. Pain exploded in Hung's skull, a blinding white flash that threatened to pull him under.

But he couldn't give in. He couldn't let them win. With the last of his strength, he twisted his body, trying to rise, but the darkness was closing in.

Just as he thought it was over, the bullies fled, their footsteps retreating down the road. Hung lay still, gasping for breath, his body a symphony of pain. Through the haze, he heard Chien's voice in his mind: *"Focus your thoughts. Find your inner strength."* He had learned so much, but there was still so much more to master. The pain was unbearable, but something deeper—something within—kept him clinging to consciousness. He wouldn't let the past defeat him.

As the world faded around him, a new thought emerged: this wasn't the end. This was only the beginning. There were more lessons to learn, more battles to fight. His journey was far from over.

Hung awoke to the sensation of being dragged across the ground. His body screamed in protest, every muscle aching as he was pulled along the dirt. His arms were folded across his chest, and a strong arm was wrapped around his waist, lifting him just enough to keep him from scraping against the earth. He tried to speak, but all that escaped his lips was a faint, broken whisper.

"Who…?"

The effort was too much, and darkness took him again.

The next time he opened his eyes, the world was still, though the pain remained. He blinked, trying to focus, the familiar scent of incense reaching his nose. The wooden walls around him stirred a distant memory. He was home. The murmur of voices broke through the fog of his thoughts, and he turned his head, wincing as the pain flared.

"He's awake," his mother's voice trembled with a mixture of relief and fear.

Beside her stood a man—a stranger to Hung, though something about him felt familiar. The man's stern face softened as he studied Hung, his piercing eyes holding a depth of recognition that made Hung's chest tighten.

"You've caused a lot of trouble, boy," the man said, his voice harsh but not unkind. "But you're lucky to be alive."

Hung struggled to make sense of the situation. His thoughts were still clouded, but one question burned in his mind. "Who are you?"

The man's expression softened further, and with a sigh, he sat beside the bed. "I'm your uncle. I've been looking for you for a long time."

The realization hit Hung like a wave. This was the family he had run from—the family he had forgotten in his search for a new life. And now that they were here, he didn't know what to feel. Relief? Guilt? Confusion?

"Why did you help me?" Hung's voice was weak, the question barely more than a rasp.

The man sighed again, his gaze softening. "Because you're family. No matter what you've done, we don't abandon our own."

Those words cut through Hung's defenses, tearing down the walls he had built around his heart. He had spent so long running from his past, but in this moment, he realized that family—real family—was something you couldn't outrun. His mother, her face streaked with tears, knelt beside him, pulling him into a tight embrace.

"We've missed you so much, Hung," she whispered, her voice breaking. "Please, don't leave us again."

And for the first time in what felt like years, Hung let the tears come. He had found a new family on the High Tides, but this—this was the family he had been born into. And despite everything, they had taken him back.

The morning light filtered through the cracks in the wooden walls, the sounds of the village stirring Hung from his sleep. He lay still for a moment, listening to the familiar clatter of pots, the distant shouts of farmers tending their fields. It was all so familiar, yet so foreign.

He had changed, and the village had stayed the same.

Dressing in the clothes his mother had left for him, Hung ate a small bowl of rice, his thoughts drifting between the past and the present. The village was no longer a cage, but neither was it his future. He had one foot in two worlds now, and the choice of which path to walk was his alone.

Stepping outside, he made his way to the river, letting the memories wash over him. He remembered the laughter and games of his childhood, the carefree days that now seemed so distant. But those memories were overshadowed by the lessons he had learned at sea, the strength he had gained under Chien's guidance.

As he stood by the river, a rustle behind him caught his attention. Turning, he saw a figure at the edge of the clearing—the boy who had saved him. Their eyes met, and for a moment, neither spoke.

"You've come a long way," the boy said finally, his voice calm, but heavy with understanding.

Hung nodded slowly, the weight of his journey settling on his shoulders. "So have you."

For a moment, they stood in silence, before the boy turned to leave.

"Wait!" Hung called after him, his heart pounding. "Who are you?"

The boy turned, a faint smile tugging at his lips. "The answer you seek lies beyond the river. But be warned, Hung—your greatest challenge is yet to come."

And with that, the boy disappeared into the trees, leaving Hung standing by the river, his mind swirling with questions. The path ahead was uncertain, but one thing was clear: his journey was far from over.

To be continued…

AFTERWORD

LITTLE DRAGON THE RECKONING

"In the heart of chaos lies the strength to rise; true transformation is forged not in the absence of fear, but in the mastery of it." —Master Wong

As we close the final pages of *"Little Dragon: The Reckoning,"* the echo of Hung Wong's extraordinary journey resonates—a narrative forged in chaos, sculpted by resilience, and transformed into something universally profound. Hung's life, once marked by the relentless sting of survival, has become a beacon for those seeking strength amidst adversity. His transformation is not just a personal evolution; it reverberates with truths about courage, identity, and the human spirit's ability to rise when faced with seemingly insurmountable odds.

Hung's path was never predictable or easy. Life threw a barrage of obstacles in his way—moments of cruelty, abandonment, and violence that could have easily shattered a lesser soul. Each punch he endured and each insult he weathered became an opportunity to sharpen his resolve, to dig deeper into the well of strength that lay within. The beatings weren't merely physical; they were battles of the mind and spirit. Through blood and bruises, Hung learned that mastery of fear was the true battlefield.

In his darkest hours, when hope seemed a distant memory, it wasn't merely the strength of muscle that carried him through—it was the quiet lessons of Knowledge Transfer **(KT)** and Tactical Training **(TT)** that his father had imparted. Hung's journey unfolded as a relentless dance between action and reflection. Each fight and every confrontation transformed into a tactical maneuver, a calculated response born from the core principles of the **KT3 system**. Whether facing down bullies in the streets or wrestling with the ghosts of his past, it was his ability to think three steps ahead and turn fear into focus that solidified his status as a survivor.

Yet, for all his tactical prowess, Hung's story transcends mere battle. It delves into the quiet, unspoken conflicts that rage within us all—the struggles of belonging, identity, and self-worth. As Hung navigated the treacherous terrain of post-war Vietnam, it was the strength discovered in his vulnerability that truly transformed him. The **Transformational Growth (TG)** he experienced was not solely about becoming a fighter; it was about rising above labels, hatred, and violence. Hung grew not only in body but in mind and spirit, learning that the most powerful weapon in his arsenal was his capacity to adapt, evolve, and rise from the ashes of each defeat.

In the heat of battle, time often slowed for Hung. Adrenaline sharpened every sense—each breath and each heartbeat felt like a countdown to something inevitable. Even as fists flew and blood stained the ground, Hung's mind calculated his next move, always learning. **Tactical Training (TT)** was not merely about fighting; it was about survival. He came to realize that survival was as much about restraint as it was about action. Hung learned that some battles were won not by overpowering an opponent but by knowing when to walk away, when to bide his time, and when to strike.

Standing at the crossroads of fear and courage, Hung's inner dialogue became his guide. The voice of his father echoed in his mind—*"Control your fear, or it will control you."* These words were more than mere advice; they were a lifeline, grounding him amid chaos. Every step he took was a calculated response to the turmoil surrounding him. Hung learned to channel his fear into focus, transforming every failure into a lesson and every defeat into a stepping stone for what lay ahead.

This relentless journey culminated in *the event that changes everything*—a moment when Hung confronted his greatest fears and emerged transformed. Hung's story serves as a reminder of the **Transformational Growth (TG)** that resides within each of us. We, like Hung, encounter battles that test our resolve. Some of these conflicts are visible—fights for survival, justice, or a place in the world—while others remain hidden, manifesting as internal struggles with doubt, fear, and uncertainty. Hung's journey invites us to reflect on our own paths, recognizing that even in our darkest moments, there exists a spark of hope and a chance for transformation.

As we conclude Hung's journey, we must remember that his story does not end here. His lessons—of courage, resilience, and the power of transformation—carry forward, reminding us that true strength is found not in victory but in the willingness to face the unknown and to persist even when the path is unclear. Hung's story teaches us that the battles we confront, though daunting, are opportunities for growth.

Every action Hung took and every fight he fought was a lesson in **Knowledge Transfer (KT)**. The wisdom passed down from his father and mentors encompassed not just the mechanics of fighting but also the art of living. It illustrated how to navigate a chaotic world and find one's center. The **Tactical Training (TT)** he absorbed transcended mere muscle memory; it became a way of perceiving the world as a series of opportunities and threats, learning to respond with precision and wisdom.

Ultimately, Hung's journey stands as a testament to **Transformational Growth (TG)**. Through each struggle, he became stronger—not just in his ability to defend himself but in his understanding of his identity and values. At the heart of Hung's story lies a rhythm of resilience and a pulse of hope, intricately woven into the fabric of his being.

As you close this book, we hope you carry with you the essence of Hung's journey. His story is a poignant reminder that even in our darkest hours, we hold the power to rise. We possess the strength to transform our pain into power, our fear into focus, and our doubts into determination. Each battle presents an opportunity to learn, grow, and evolve.

In the end, Hung's story is not solely his; it is ours. It is a call to face our struggles with courage and to embrace the transformation that resides within each of us. The conclusion of this book marks not the end of the journey but the beginning of something new. For Hung, for us, and for all who dare to rise above life's trials, the reckoning has only just begun.

CONGRATULATIONS

Congratulations on finishing *Little Dragon: The Reckoning*! You've been through an inspiring journey of resilience, transformation, and mastery. But here's the real question:

What's next?
Have you ever felt stuck—unsure of how to move forward? It's your time to take control of your life, just as Hung did. **Imagine yourself** unlocking the same mastery, using the KT3 System to achieve success.

What if you could...
Absorb life-changing wisdom that empowers you to tackle any obstacle?

Train with precision, sharpening both your body and mind to become unstoppable?
Grow continuously, turning challenges into opportunities for success?

The KT3 System will guide you:
Knowledge Transfer (KT): Gain clarity and direction through powerful strategies.

Tactical Training (TT): Build the discipline and resilience to handle any challenge.

Transformational Growth (TG): Evolve into your strongest self—mentally, physically, and spiritually.

What if you could master every situation with confidence and clarity? The path to that transformation is already open.

The time to act is now. By joining our KT3 Training Program, you'll experience personalized mentorship, blending ancient wisdom with modern strategy. **Limited spaces are available**, so don't wait!

Don't wait—Contact us now
at www.kt3system.com

To start your KT3 journey.

Spaces are limited, and your transformation is only one call away for your free consultation.

"The way you do anything is the way you do everything. True mastery comes from mastering the mind, body, and spirit." — *Master Wong*

THE 3 MASTERS
FORGING THE PATH TO MASTERY

Three Masters. One Journey. Infinite Wisdom.

Master Chien – The Strategist and Warrior
Master Chien, a veteran resistance fighter from the Vietnam War, instills in Hung a deep understanding of **discipline**, **strategy**, and the strength of both mind and body. Under his rigorous training, Hung learns **Wing Chun**, a close-combat martial art that emphasizes swift, efficient movements and sharp reactions. This practical art of self-defense sharpens Hung's reflexes and physical resilience.

In addition to martial arts, Master Chien teaches Hung the art of **guerrilla warfare** and **survival tactics**—key skills honed during his time as a resistance fighter. These lessons train Hung to stay adaptable in combat, to anticipate an enemy's moves, and to thrive in harsh conditions. Through Chien, Hung learns not only how to fight, but also how to endure.

Master Chien also introduces Hung to **The Art of War** by **Sun Tzu**, grounding his teachings in strategy and war tactics. The philosophy of winning without fighting, of knowing when to strike and when to retreat, becomes deeply embedded in Hung's mind. Alongside this, Chien pushes Hung's **fitness** and **body conditioning** to new limits, ensuring his body is as strong and flexible as his mind. These lessons form the foundation of Hung's transformation into **Master Wong**, where discipline and sharp awareness become key tools in overcoming life's greatest challenges.

Master Linh – The Healer and Balance Seeker
Master Linh introduces Hung to a softer, yet equally powerful side of mastery—**emotional balance**, **healing**, and **harmony**. Her teachings focus on **Daoist philosophy**, particularly the wisdom of **Laozi**, and the practice of **Wu Wei**—the art of effortless action. Under her guidance, Hung learns that mastery comes not only through physical strength but through the **inner peace** that comes from aligning with nature.

Linh trains Hung in **Tai Chi**, a slow and meditative martial art that blends movement with breath, allowing him to flow with the world around him. Through her, Hung discovers the concept of **Yin-Yang balance**, both in combat and in life. She also imparts knowledge of **holistic health**, including **Yin-Yang nutrition**, teaching Hung how food, rest, and mindfulness all contribute to physical and emotional well-being.

With her expertise in **meditation**, Linh helps Hung manage stress, develop mental clarity, and foster emotional control. Her teachings show him the power of **inner stillness** in overcoming external chaos. This balance is crucial as Hung prepares to navigate the path from student to Master Wong, where staying calm and centered will be as important as any martial skill.

Master Lee – The Strategist and Entrepreneur
Master Lee brings a unique blend of wisdom, drawing from both his past as a former Triad gangster and his transformation into a respected mentor and strategist. Through him, Hung learns **leadership**, **business acumen**, and **strategic decision-making**. Lee's guidance takes Hung beyond combat, into the realms of **entrepreneurship** and **ethical leadership**, teaching him how to apply the principles of strategy in everyday life.

One of Lee's greatest contributions to Hung's growth is his instruction in **neurology**, helping Hung understand the connection between brain function and behavior. Lee also teaches Hung **numerology** and the **I Ching**, showing him how to use these ancient systems of wisdom to better understand patterns in life and make informed, intuitive decisions. These mystical and intellectual tools deepen Hung's understanding of the **mind's potential**.

Master Lee intertwines his teachings with the strategic insights of **Sun Tzu** and the **I Ching**, helping Hung develop long-term vision, resilience in the face of uncertainty, and the ability to lead others with integrity. Lee's emphasis on **planning**, **timing**, and **ethical action** forms the final layer of Hung's training, preparing him to become a leader not just in martial arts, but in all areas of life.

The Birth of the KT3 System
Through the combined wisdom of his three masters, Hung evolves into **Master Wong** and creates the **KT3 System**—a transformative framework built on the three pillars of **Knowledge Transfer (KT)**, **Tactical Training (TT)**, and **Transformational Growth (TG)**. The KT3 System is more than just a martial arts program; it is a **complete philosophy of life**, blending **Wing Chun**, **Daoist philosophy**, **numerology**, and **strategic leadership** into a cohesive system that helps individuals master not only their bodies, but their minds and spirits.

The KT3 System reflects Hung's personal journey and the teachings that shaped him. It offers a roadmap for others to conquer their own challenges, helping them find the balance between action and stillness, strategy and intuition, and resilience and adaptability. In *The 3 Master*, readers will see how these principles are applied in life and combat, equipping them with the tools they need to grow into their own mastery.

Prepare for the Next Step…
The 3 Master takes readers deeper into Hung's transformation, revealing the powerful lessons that shaped him into **Master Wong** and birthed the KT3 System. Through the wisdom of **guerrilla warfare, self-defense, Wu Wei, neurology, and more**, readers will discover how to apply these principles to their own lives, turning obstacles into opportunities for growth. This is not just a continuation of the *Little Dragon* series—it's an invitation to embark on the journey of personal mastery.

Available Soon.

MASTER WONG

IS THE FOUNDER OF
KT3 SYSTEM

TEACHING PHILOSOPHY AND IMPACT

Master Wong's philosophy blends traditional martial arts with modern self-defense, infused with Ying-Yang Nutrition and strategic insights from Laozi and Sun Tzu. His teachings extend far beyond combat, emphasizing character building through the 12 Virtues (WuDe)—instilling consistency, commitment, and adaptability.

As chronicled in his autobiographical book, Little Dragon: The Reckoning, Master Wong's rise from adversity in Vietnam to becoming a global martial arts authority is a testament to the transformative power of martial arts. From his base in Ipswich, England, Master Wong shares these teachings with a global audience, offering individuals the opportunity to transform their lives through the KT3 System.

The KT3 System:
Created in honor of his three mentors—Master Chien, Master Linh, and Master Lee—the KT3 System combines Knowledge Transfer (KT), Tactical Training (TT), and Transformational Growth (TG). These pillars reflect Master Wong's holistic approach, blending martial arts, strategic thinking, and wellness for comprehensive personal growth.

Master Chien's Legacy: Shaped by Master Chien's teachings on strategic thinking and mental resilience, the KT3 System emphasizes clear thinking and adaptability in all situations.

Master Linh's Legacy: Known for her focus on holistic healing and balance, Master Linh's principles form the foundation of KT3's wellness aspect, emphasizing the connection between mind, body, and spirit.

Master Lee's Legacy: Master Lee's focus on Sun Tzu's strategies, Daoist philosophy, numerology, and neurological insights informs the strategic and mental aspects of the KT3 mentorship, guiding students toward profound personal mastery. Numerology adds another layer to the mentorship, helping students understand patterns and make informed decisions based on the significance of numbers in their personal and professional journeys.

Master Wong Today:
With a global digital following of millions, Master Wong continues to inspire and transform lives through the KT3 System. His mentorship helps individuals not only master martial arts but also health, wealth, and relationships—equipping them with the tools to navigate life's complexities with confidence and strength.

Are you ready to begin your own transformation? Discover the power of the KT3 System by joining the thousands who have already experienced its life-changing impact. Contact us today to learn how KT3 can help you master every aspect of your life.

"Mastery is not found in defeating others, but in conquering the battles within. When you rise above fear, pain, and doubt, you discover the true strength that has always been yours." — Master Wong

I would love to hear what you've learned on your journey with Hung and how it has inspired you Contact me directly using the QR code:

KT3 FaceBook Page

A Journey of Learning and Sharing Across the World

Throughout my years of teaching and mentoring martial artists globally, I've had the honor of meeting many incredible masters, teachers, and grandmasters. Each encounter has deepened my understanding of martial arts, life, and personal growth. One such master, known as the Pit Master, has become like a big brother to me—his wisdom, strength, and guidance have had a profound impact on my journey.

Below are photos from the various events and seminars I've held and attended around the world, where I continue to learn as much as I teach. Each moment is a testament to the lifelong journey of mastery, not just in martial arts, but in how we approach life itself.

Master Wong
Sharing KT3 in USA
Master Wong
Sharing KT3 in Hanoi, Vietnam Wing Chun

Master Wong
Sharing KT3 in UK
Master Wong
Sharing KT3 in USA
Master Wong
Sharing KT3 in UK

Master Wong
Sharing KT3 in Ha Long Bay, Vietnam

Master Wong
Sharing KT3 in Hanoi, Vietnam

KUNGFU CENTER - VĨNH XUÂN THĂNG LONG
Master Wong
KT3 System
Wing Chun Master
Dinh Trong Thuy

GLOSSARY

Agent Orange: A powerful herbicide used by the U.S. military during the Vietnam War to eliminate forest cover and crops. It caused serious health issues and environmental damage.

Ammonia: A strong, pungent-smelling chemical often found in urine. The smell of ammonia in the alley reflects the unsanitary conditions Hung often finds himself in.

Boat People: A term used to describe the Vietnamese refugees who fled the country by boat after the Vietnam War, often facing dangerous and life-threatening conditions.

Buffalo Stink: A term used by Hung to describe the strong, unpleasant odor of the water buffaloes he tends in the rice fields.

China Sea: A marginal sea that is part of the Pacific Ocean, situated near Vietnam. It is a key geographical location in the book, representing both a barrier and a potential escape route for refugees like Hung's family.

Demons: Used metaphorically in the book to describe the internal fears and external threats that haunt Hung throughout his journey.

Exodus: Refers to the mass departure of people from Vietnam during and after the Vietnam War, driven by the fear of persecution and the desire for a better life.

Flotsam: Refers to the floating debris found in the sea, which Hung's mother scavenges in the hope of finding valuable items.

Half-Breed: A derogatory term used to describe someone of mixed race, particularly in the context of Hung's Vietnamese and Chinese heritage, which isolates him and his family in their community.

Ha Long Bay: A UNESCO World Heritage site in Quảng Ninh Province, Vietnam, known for its emerald waters and thousands of towering limestone islands. It serves as a geographical anchor in the book, representing both beauty and danger.

Internal Growth: Refers to Hung's psychological and emotional development as he faces the challenges of his harsh environment. This growth is part of his Transformational Growth (TG), a key principle in the KT3 System.

KT3 System: A conceptual framework in the book that stands for Knowledge Transfer (KT), Tactical Training (TT), and Transformational Growth (TG). These principles guide Hung's development throughout the narrative.

Linh (Master Linh): A significant figure in Hung's life who teaches him important lessons about resilience and strength, particularly in the face of physical and emotional pain.

Mandela, Nelson: A South African anti-apartheid revolutionary and political leader quoted in the book. His words about rising every time one falls resonate with Hung's journey.

Nón Lá: A traditional Vietnamese conical hat, often worn by farmers and rural workers for protection from the sun.

Pacing: In the context of storytelling, pacing refers to the speed at which the narrative unfolds. The book's pacing varies to reflect the intensity of Hung's experiences.

Psycho: A nickname given to one of the bullies in the book, reflecting his violent and unpredictable nature.

Reckoning: A term that signifies a moment of truth or judgment. In the book, it refers to Hung's critical confrontations with both his inner demons and external threats.

Survival: A central theme in the book, referring to Hung's continuous struggle to stay alive and protect his family in a hostile environment.

Slim: One of the antagonists in the book, known for his lean build and cruel demeanor.

Tactical Training (TT): A component of the KT3 System, focusing on the strategic skills Hung develops to survive and outmaneuver his enemies.

Vietnam War: A conflict that took place from 1955 to 1975, involving Vietnam, Laos, and Cambodia, with major influence from the United States and other global powers. The war's aftermath plays a significant role in the backdrop of Hung's story.

Wong Family: The central family in the book, of which Hung is a member. Their mixed Chinese-Vietnamese heritage sets them apart and makes them targets of persecution.

Xenophobia: An irrational fear or dislike of people from other countries. This concept is evident in the book through the discrimination and violence faced by Hung's family due to their mixed heritage.

Yen Tu Mountain: A mountain in northern Vietnam, historically significant as a center for Buddhist teaching and practice. It is not directly mentioned in the book but represents the kind of natural environment Hung might have encountered.

Zenith: The highest point, representing the peak of Hung's struggles and growth. In the narrative, it symbolizes the moments where Hung's internal and external battles come to a head.

YOUR JOURNEY BEGINS HERE!

Thank you for joining me on this journey. Hung's story is one of transformation, and I hope it has inspired you to reflect on your own potential and strength. Remember, no matter where you start, with belief and the right guidance, you can achieve anything.

I would love to hear about your experience with the book—what did you learn, and how has it impacted you? Please take a moment to leave a review on Amazon and share your thoughts on social media. Your feedback means everything to me and helps others discover this story.

To show my gratitude, if you leave a review on Amazon and contact me directly through my Facebook page or Youtube, I will send you a 14 day training program to help you get started on your own journey toward mastery using the KT3 System.

Connect with me on Facebook, leave a review, and let's take the next step together!

Contact me directly using the QR code:
KT3 FaceBook Page

AS YOU CONCLUDE THE JOURNEY!

Remember, this journey is not simply an end but a call to continuous mastery.

Believe in the power within you.
Act with the purity of your intent.
Hold steadfast in the focus of your will.
Embrace the depth of your awareness.
Honor the quality of your character.

Carry these pillars forward, for mastery is not a destination but a way of life.
—Master Wong

"Remember, true mastery is not only in the self but in what we pass on to those we love."

www.ingramcontent.com/pod-product-compliance
Lightning Source LLC
Chambersburg PA
CBHW051547030726
47592CB00001B/173